9780853403579

D1743238

The Piccadilly
World of Golf
1973-74

Tom Weiskopf – Open Champion and defending title-holder in the 1973 Piccadilly World Match-play Championship.

The Piccadilly World of Golf 1973–74

Compiled and edited by
Golf World Magazine

Contributors

Bob Ferrier
Peter Dobereiner
Ben Wright
Henry Longhurst
Geoffrey Cotton
John Jacobs
Geoffrey Cousins
Dan Jenkins
Mike Stevenson
Ray Jacobs
Iain Crawford
Pam Brassington
George Houghton
Ken Adwick

WAYLAND PUBLISHERS LONDON

SBN 85340 357 0
Copyright © 1973 by
Golf World Magazine Limited and Wayland Publishers Limited
First published in 1973 by Wayland Publishers Limited
101 Grays Inn Road, London W.C.1
Printed by Jarrold & Sons Ltd, Norwich

Foreword

George Hammond

*CHAIRMAN OF THE PICCADILLY
WORLD MATCH-PLAY
CHAMPIONSHIP COMMITTEE*

Golf is rapidly becoming one of our most popular sports and with its unique attraction for the highly talented and the beginner alike, its devotees increase every day.

Sponsorship in sport is here to stay and golf certainly gets its fair share of commercial involvement. It has been said in the past that this would be to the detriment of the game, but happily it has proved to be the reverse.

Industrial sponsors have contributed a great deal to providing an opportunity for enthusiasts to see, both on television and on the course, the best the sport has to offer. Since 1962, The House of Piccadilly has been one of the main sponsors of golf, both in the professional and amateur fields, and the Piccadilly World Match-play Championship, now in its tenth year, is one of the established world class tournaments. It has brought pleasure to millions through the medium of television and film.

In 1972 we produced the first edition of the *Piccadilly World of Golf*, and such was its popularity that this year we have published a second edition packed with illustrated articles and features full of interest for everyone. We hope the book will once again provide enjoyment for all golfers whatever their handicap.

Contents

I

The Piccadilly World Match-play Championship

by Bob Ferrier

member of the Piccadilly World Match-play
Championship Committee

What's so special about the Piccadilly World Match-play Championship?

What makes it so clearly different from almost every other golf tournament in its appeal, so that in the minds of most British golf writers – a hard-nosed school – it is second only to the Open Championship in its recurring dramas and compelling public interest?

These are difficult questions to answer, and almost all the suggested answers will be subjective at best, hopelessly biased at worst. Yet there is very little doubt that the World Match-play Championship is one of the great success stories in international golf. In 1973 it went into its tenth year, and almost every single one of these years has thrown up something extraordinary. Ten years is a long time for any commercially sponsored event to survive, particularly with the same format and at the same venue over that time, for all commercial companies are constantly seeking the new and the different and the exclusive. But from its very first year, the World Match-play took a clear hold on the affections of the British golfing public and there is no indication that this is lessening in the slightest. The public has supported the event so passionately that they have forced us to abandon admissions at the gate on the day, so that the World Match-play had to become the first British tournament to have advance ticket sales only, and the first British tournament to put a daily limit on attendance.

Our experience with the event indicates that the old saw, "you can't buy success", does have a fair slice of truth to it. Companies much richer, more powerful than ours, have gone into golf promotion offering huge purses and incurring lavish expenditures, and concluded that their efforts have failed to get the required results.

Scheduling is an increasing problem in international golf. The South African circuit is growing. The Australian and Far East circuit is growing. And the Japanese "domestic" circuit is growing about as fast as their electronic or automobile industries are growing and when you consider all that against the foundation of the U.S. circuit, with more than 40 major events scheduled each year for a total of more than $7,000,000 you will see that there are just too many golf tournaments chasing too few weeks in the year. All this is money-in-the-bank for the players and some think they are spoiled. But one can hardly indict them for accepting all this largesse.

In trying to assess the World Match-play,

Piccadilly World Match-play champion 1972 – TOM WEISKOPF. *He defeated* LEE TREVINO *four and three in the final.*

ARNOLD PALMER, *winner of the first Piccadilly World Match-play Championship in 1964 when he was taken to the 35th hole by* NEIL COLES.

one might be driven to the conclusion that it has all been a matter of chemistry – and that the chemistry somehow worked out right. But specific points can be made. Most important of all was probably the format. The concept was that the eight best players in the world during the year – in our judgment – including the winners of the world's major championships, would be invited to compete in 36-holes elimination match-play. The fact that over the years the world's best players have seen this concept as attractive and challenging to them is a small miracle in itself. Their life-style is four rounds of medal play, the 72-holes stroke-play competition. They are wholly conditioned to this everywhere in the world and their performances are geared to it – the rhythm of their work from week to week relates to four days of play, 18 holes each day so that they can com-

fortably accept the birdies as they come, or absorb the small disasters as they come, with time for repairs to their form, or contemplation, between rounds.

Not so in match-play. In match-play you live or die from day to day. In medal play, oddly, no one loses. There is a winner, and everyone else finishes relative to him – second, 12th, 25th, 49th. Match-play is the contrary. Everyone loses except the winner, and heads fall every day. So it was both surprising and gratifying that the great players of the world were prepared to have a go, put their pride up to auction, put their heads on the block. Even more surprising was the fact that they were prepared to handle 36 holes each day, over a long (7,000 yards) course in the English autumn. Finalists in our tournament must play most of six rounds over three days – severe physical demands on a man

12

GARY PLAYER, *the man who has dominated the Piccadilly event, winning the title in 1965, 1966, 1968 and again in 1971.*

who faces the tension of tackling opponents of his own steel all that time. Few of the players, if the truth be known, like 36 holes in a day. But they have all accepted it.

As Peter Thomson once said, after losing a final to Arnold Palmer, "The compensation is satisfactory." The fact that we have a small and distinguished field of eight players has meant that we could do much more for them individually than could any sponsor with a field of, say, 120. We have always sought to compensate them not in cash terms alone. We have sought to take care of their transportation problems. Each player on arrival in London is met by a chauffeur-driven limousine, which is at his personal disposal until the end of the tournament. The players have a private restaurant at Wentworth, a private dressing-room with service and massage staff.

In the early years, the players were lodged in the Carlton Tower Hotel in London, then quite new and on the "right" side of the city for Wentworth. Then it was thought that the hotel, although excellent, was too "American" in character and that an English hotel might be more attractive to these world travellers. So for many years, each player had a River Suite at the Savoy, and for those of you who may not have seen one, I can tell you that they are passably comfortable. In time, the drive from the Savoy to Wentworth, some 25 miles against the commuter traffic both morning and evening, became irksome. We thought of alternatives – a special railway car from Waterloo, even a helicopter, which was arranged one year. In the event, only two players used it once during the entire week. To solve the travel problem, we moved the

13

players to the course. Now each player has a secluded rented house in the Wentworth-Ascot area, within a few miles of the course, and each with a complete staff, including a "cordon bleu" cook, for the week.

Thus events and organisations evolve. We learned, for example, that we could "over-entertain" our guests. We learned that there are times when players' wives prefer to potter around London on their own. And I suppose above all that over the years we have learned that in organising a major sports event like the World Match-play, it is the small things that can kill you, and that although the years create their own library of experience, one must constantly work at the organisation, constantly try to improve the small things, in particular where they relate to spectator facilities. Information on the course is very important, and we have worked hard on our scoring systems in spite of the fact that match-play poses particular problems in this respect. We may have been first to provide on-course transport for spectators, running bus and car services from the car parks and clubhouse areas to the action. Our cinema, showing golf films, has been a notable success. We have worked hard on public catering, with the problem, exclusive to match-play, that the action stops in the middle of the day, and everyone wants to eat at the same time – within an hour!

Crowd control in the early years made for headaches and eventually a restriction on total numbers became essential and the entire course had to be fenced. Arnold Palmer used to say that we were not allow-ing the crowd enough room to move – admittedly on a tight course – and that we should move the fences further in, narrowing even more Wentworth's slender fairways. "Hell, the players won't mind," he'd say. Yet no tournament has more faithful follow-

ers, hundreds of fans reappearing year after year from all corners of the kingdom. The fact that we are in London in a period when the golf fans of Southern England have no chance to see the game's supermen in action in the living flesh probably accounts for this loyalty. And the fact that as a matter of policy we have stayed at Wentworth gives the event a rare continuity, providing people with the chance to compare the shot that Nicklaus played at the 13th hole with the shot that Palmer played from the same place a few years before. The West Course at Wentworth, like everything else regarding the tournament over the years, has had its critics, but the executives of the club have heard it all before and pay it no mind, for they know that their course has this criticism in common with every great golf course in the world, from the Old Course down. Wentworth dry, as it has been during the tournament, can be a fiery monster, hard to control. Wentworth wet, as it has been too, can be a heavyweight slog. But again in com-mon with all great golf courses, if you play good, correct shots, it will reward you abundantly. If you play bad, ill-advised shots, it will destroy you. Above all, it never lets a player relent. That is as a course should be.

Television has been a very critical factor in making the World Match-play what it is. The televising of golf is difficult. The arena extends over more than 100 acres. The amount of highly sophisticated, hugely expensive equipment needed is formidable. Then again match-play poses particular problems for the producer. Not yet has tech-nology permitted him to cover all 18 holes of a golf course, or every shot played every-where by every player. Six or seven holes of coverage is the norm, but in match-play, who can say where any match may end? So two

The late TONY LEMA *was involved in one of the Piccadilly World Match-play Championship classics. Seven up on* PLAYER *with 17 holes to play in the semi-final of 1965 he was beaten on the 37th green.*

through the first round, had to go 37 holes against Christie O'Connor, ailing from "flu", with the match suspended at the 36th because of darkness, and with the one extra hole played early the following morning.

The first day in 1966 produced two remarkable first-18 efforts. Palmer against Roberto de Vicenzo scored 66 and was five up. Nicklaus against David Thomas scored 64 and was five up. Gary Player, defending his title, beat on successive days Neil Coles one up, Arnold Palmer 2 and 1, then in the final Jack Nicklaus by 6 and 4 – a fair week's work. If Player, in fact, was determined to put his stamp on the championship, he certainly succeeded. In 1967, again defending his title, he drew Gay Brewer, the contemporary U.S. Masters Champion, in the first round. Brewer came up with a morning 67 to be three up. Player responded with an afternoon 69 to tie the match, Brewer having to hole from about 10 feet on the 36th green to stay alive. They went into extra holes, halving the 37th in birdies, the 38th in pars. Then at the 39th, the third extra hole, Brewer noticed that the hole had been cut in a different part of the green, in preparation for the following day's play. He insisted they play to the original hole, and in the gathering twilight this was done. The hole was re-cut in its original position – it was a decision still good for a long clubhouse argument – but it turned to Gay's disadvantage. He lost the hole, and the match.

Gary Player just could not be kept out of the headlines in the World Match-play. In 1968, Tony Jacklin appeared on the scene for the first time, and disposing of another debutante, Lee Trevino, fairly comfortably on day one, by 4 and 3, he faced Gary in the semi-final. They went at it in a dour and rather untidy match, which went to the 37th where Player, again, won when Jacklin

17

three-putted in controversial circumstances. Player went on to beat Bob Charles in the final by one meagre hole. The following year he racked up the tournament's biggest margin in beating Jean Garaialde of France by 10 and 8 in a first-round match. Then in the semi-final against the impeccable Gene Littler, Player got the other end of the stick when the American reeled off seven successive threes at him, from the fifth to the tenth hole in the morning round, scoring 65. The final that year also added a little more to the tournament's history – Bob Charles prevailed at the 37th hole over Littler after one of the most bewildering exhibitions of putting, from all ranges, surely ever seen anywhere. In 1970 Jacklin had some kind of revenge in beating Gary Player in a first-round match of moderate quality, but the tournament highlight this year was Nicklaus against the surging Trevino in the final. Nicklaus was five up with only nine to play when Trevino got him by the throat. Only when Trevino, back to one down, hit an over-audacious tee shot at the 35th, which went marginally out of bounds, did Nicklaus pin him down, 2 and 1. It was the gallant thrust that failed, but even that was sur-

passed by Trevino's match with Jacklin in 1972. Then, Jacklin was four down after 18, but played the first nine at Wentworth in the afternoon in 29 strokes, and went one up! Once more in historic British fashion it was the counter that failed, but the match went all the way to the 36th hole when at lunch time it had looked comfortably over.

All of this has been the stuff of history, and manna for the media. Most great sports events have longevity and history on their side. The Cup Final is the Cup Final regardless of the teams involved from year to year. The Derby, Wimbledon, the Open, the Lord's Test are inviolable. I don't mean to compare the World Match-play with these events. But certainly it seems true that in 10 short years it has created a unique place for itself in the heart of the British golf public. I believe ultimately that its success has been due to the quality of the talent competing, and to match-play itself. The public, it seems, cannot resist the factor of man against man and one winner, one loser – and the loser goes home.

Whatever it is, the Piccadilly World Match-play Championship has its own certain style, its own certain flavour.

2

The Lighter Side of Life on Tour

by Peter Dobereiner

Perhaps it is the advance of old age, just another symptom of the policemen looking younger, the traffic wardens prettier and the jokes in *Punch* getting even duller, but it seems to me that life on the golf circuit has lost some of its sparkle.

Inevitable, I suppose, with so much money at stake. The young pros are serious and a bit too dedicated for their own good, at times. There seem to be no characters coming into the game, not in the grand style of Max Faulkner or Tommy Bolt. Even the caddies have become as respectable as chartered accountants. It was not so long ago when the beer tent would be carpeted two deep with drunken caddies. These days they stand around discussing the movement of the stock market.

Will we ever again see the like of Mad Mac, for instance? He carried for Faulkner and would have made a splendid music-hall turn. Winter or summer, he wore a selection of top coats. Beneath these layers he sported several ties but no shirt. His speciality was a pair of opera glasses from which the lenses had long since vanished. He used to peer through this bizarre instrument at the line of a putt and then deliver solemn judgment: "Hit it slightly straight, sir."

And then there was Little Mac, who caddied for Dai Rees for some time and whom I was glad to see bobbing and weaving among the crowd at a recent tournament. Standing side by side, Little Mac made Dai Rees look like a giant and it did not take much beer to top up the wee fellow. And when he had his ration aboard, Little Mac feared no man. At the slightest provocation he would put up his fists and I imagine he took a bit of handling. It would be like fighting a frenzied garden gnome.

At the time when he was in his prime the travelling caddies were not too fussy about their sleeping arrangements. If they couldn't find a boarding house with a convenient back window they slept rough. One night Little Mac found the perfect spot. The tournament was over and he crept between the folds of a dismantled tent. Came the dawn and the contractor's men folded the tent and loaded it onto their lorry, with Little Mac still peacefully sleeping inside like the meat in a sausage roll.

The era of the vagabond caddie really ended with the Battle of the Nineteenth Hole, which I should explain is a pub at St. Andrews. Two enterprising caddies went to Prestwick to meet the aircraft bringing over two famous American golfers. They politely touched their caps and announced boldly: "We are your caddies." They took charge of the bags.

However, on arrival at St. Andrews the golfers discovered that two quite different caddies had been booked for them. The arrangements had been made some weeks in advance. So the men who had gone to Prestwick had to give up the bags and, at this late juncture, they were unable to find work for that week. They just had to sit this one out. Their hard-luck stories generated considerable sympathy among the fraternity of caddies and at the end of the tournament a meeting was held in the Nineteenth Hole.

"Brothers," said the spokesman, "through no fault of their own two of our colleagues have been unable to work this week. I would like to pass a motion through the chair that a collection be taken up forthwith on their behalf." So saying, a hat was passed and generously filled. The two beneficiaries silently trousered the loot, too overcome to trust themselves to speak.

It was an incident to touch the heart. Who could fail to be moved by such an example of brotherhood? Who indeed? The caddies who had actually carried the Americans' bags slipped quietly into the night.

They presented themselves at the hotel of their employers and recounted the events of that evening.

"Since Americans are famed – and justly so – for their legendary generosity, we thought you would like to know of an act of generosity on our part. Those two poor caddies who met you at Prestwick will be all right after all. As you know, they had no work but we have seen to it that their wives and children shall not starve. From the

Colourful characters like MAX FAULKNER, *Open Champion in 1951, are sadly missed on today's golf tour.*

generous fees which you paid us, we in our part have donated a proportion – a goodly proportion, even if we say so ourselves – to those two unfortunates. It matters not that our own families will have to subsist on potato stew. The bailiffs will just have to get on with their work. We shall all scrape by, somehow. The most important thing is that you shall not return to America with those two men on your consciences. We just wanted you to know, you being compassionate men and noted for your own generosity, even though the sums involved would seem so paltry to wealthy men like yourselves that you would not even notice it.''

"We are,'' replied the golfers, ''duly moved, even unto tears, by this tale of charity. There is, however, one small point which you should know. Those two men who were unable to work did not go unrewarded. We paid them in full, at the top rates. Now be so kind as to get the hell out of here you conniving, cadging bums.''

The caddies returned to the Nineteenth Hole in pensive mood and in some haste. And when they told the assembled company what they had learned the room was filled with wrath. And flying bottles. And boots. And fists. And when the dust finally settled no pane of glass remained intact in the windows. Life on the caddie circuit has never been the same since.

With that kind of opposition, it is difficult for a mere golfer to make much impact on the comic lore of the game. But there are moments, notably one in the Bahamas when a player shanked his nine-iron approach and

Milwaukee postal worker WALTER DANECKI *falsely entered himself for the Open in 1965 as a professional – then scored 108 and 113 in the qualifying rounds.*

hurled his club in anger. Since golf is played sideways he was, you will appreciate, facing the rough at the critical moment and it was therefore in this direction that the guilty club was dispatched.

I lay particular stress on this point since it underlines the validity of the argument that if you must chuck clubs you should always hurl them in the direction of play. It saves extra walking. This player forgot that cardinal rule and he failed to take into due consideration the nature of the rough. On the Bahamian courses it consists of the thickest, lushest tropical jungle you can imagine.

Search as they might, the golfer and his playing partner could find no sign of the nine-iron. One of golf's oldest jokes is that in such circumstances the player wails: "What can I do now?" and his partner replies: "Go back and throw another." This, more or less, is exactly what they decided to do. The player said to his partner: "You go and stand in the jungle. I will throw another club from the same spot so you will be able to mark where it lands. Then we will surely find the nine-iron in the same spot."

The theory of the plan was unsound but it could have worked. The player returned to the spot and a moment later the marker standing in the jungle heard the crash of a two-iron among the branches. He heard but did not see. Neither club was ever recovered.

Deliberate practical jokes on the golf course are rare these days, although in the not so distant past we had a long-running serial story. Discretion forbids me to reveal the names of the three illustrious golfers involved. The idea was to create the maximum embarrassment to each other and this was achieved by hiding a small article of maximum blush-making potential.

Let us say it was a pair of panties. This was called "Noddy" and the rules were simple. The intended victim was simply informed "Noddy hidden." Thus it was that a famous player would step onto the tee for an exhibition match, in front of a thousand people, and as he pulled the head-cover from his driver Noddy would flutter to the ground.

These days the number one joker is undoubtedly Jimmy Kinsella. His fun consists of throwing out challenges over feats of strength and athleticism. In a practice round I once saw him challenge David Vaughan to a hundred-yard sprint up the fairway, the handicap being that Kinsella should pull his trolley. And he won.

Another time he took a wager that he could leap a hedge, which looked difficult enough, but proved a great deal harder when, in mid air, he saw that there was a wide ditch on the blind side.

The funniest experience I ever had on a golf course was at the U.S. Open at Baltusrol. I should explain that while we in Britain have caravan toilets, fitted with every mod. con., the American practice is to dot the course with individual privvies, like sentry boxes.

With Arnold Palmer paired with Jack Nicklaus, almost the entire gallery followed that one match. Such is the foresight and detailed planning at an American Open that, once the players had moved onto the sixth tee, an official ordered that the privvies by the fourth fairway should be transferred to the 16th hole.

LITTLE MAC, *who caddied for* DAI REES *for many years, came out of retirement to pull a trolley for American* BILL HYNDMAN *during the British Amateur at Carnoustie in 1966.*

It is that kind of thinking which has made America great. The man who anticipates public demand, and is on the spot with the goods, makes the million. A lorry trundled round and four burly groundsmen hoisted one, two, three privvies aboard. As they raised the fourth a scream rent the air. They lowered it again. There was a flurry within the cabinet and then emerged a lady, puce with embarrassment, who fled for the sanctuary of the trees like a frightened gazelle.

Finally, no review of the lighter side of golf would be complete without some mention of Walter Danecki, who was a postal sorter in Milwaukee and a golf nut. He had played golf on his local municipal course for a few years and by 1965 felt he was ready to tackle the big boys. He had decided to vacation in Britain and thought it would give the folks back home a kick if he returned as British Open champion. So he sent in his entry and described himself as a professional.

That was not quite true. He had tried to become a proper pro but the U.S.P.G.A. wouldn't accept him until he had served a five-year apprenticeship. Walter thought they would have to let him in if he won the Open. Besides, he wanted the money. "My conscience made me write down professional," he said.

Walter's first round over Royal Birkdale in the qualifying contest was 108. Nobody expected him to have the gall to turn up next day but Walter came. "I don't like to quit," he said. He went round in 113, for a total of 43 over par, and then made his dignified exit with the curtain line: "If I had been playing our bigger ball I would have been all over the place."

Tom Weiskopf, winner of the 1973 Piccadilly World Match-Play Championship. He disposed of David Graham by three and two in the first round, Peter Oosterhuis by four and three in the semi-final and Lee Trevino by the same margin over the final 36 holes.

Lee Trevino at St. Andrews – golf's brash superstar at the decorous home of golf. Trevino, whose superlative golf game has earned him championship titles and wealth throughout the world and whose spontaneous wit and non-stop chatter has captivated golf audiences, this year passed 1,000,000 dollars in prize-money.

Peter Oosterhuis leapt to prominence by finishing third in the American Masters at Augusta. His consistency of performance had already won him the Harry Vardon Trophy for the best stroke average on the British circuit in 1971 and 1972.

Ryder Cup captain Bernard Hunt discusses a fine point with Britain's star performer Tony Jacklin. The 1973 match against America at Muirfield attracted the biggest crowd ever to have watched the outcome of the Ryder Cup contest.

It was fitting that Tommy Aaron's first major championship victory should have been at Augusta National in the U.S. Masters, for it was on this golf course, in the same event, that he watched his boyhood hero, Ben Hogan.

Dawn on the final day of the Open Championship at St. Andrews – and as the sun first strikes the grey stone façade of the Royal and Ancient Golf Club there is no hint of the incredible crowd scenes that will greet the new holder of the Open title in a few hours' time.

Gary Player is more concerned with the outcome of his shot at Spain's new La Manga complex than the fact that the shaft of his club has snapped at impact.

3
Where is Golf Going in 1974?

by Ben Wright

Is there no end in sight to the extraordinary golf explosion that has rocked the Western world in the past decade? Certainly it seems that 1974 is destined to be another golden year for everyone commercially involved with the game. Not even the fact that it becomes less and less fun, and more of a costly, even ruinous obsession can apparently halt the golfing juggernaut. Not even a trail of broken marriages – and it is not always the husband who falls victim to what can become a disease of the mind – not even a bevy of ruined businesses, causes the infected masses to spare but a second thought as they speed like lemmings to take their places in the pre-dawn queues at our municipal courses. Far from foreseeing a levelling off of the dizzily upward spiralling golf-equipment sales graph, my crystal ball reveals very much the reverse pattern for 1974.

It also comes up with several more mildly fascinating disclosures, namely that a brilliant Russian golfer, Boris Matzoukoff, aged 19, standing but five feet seven inches tall, and weighing a handy $11\frac{1}{2}$ stone, has just broken 70 for the 32nd successive time behind locked doors, as it were, on a 7,300-yard-long course hacked out of the foothills

of the Urals. Latest reports of Matzoukoff's progress indicate that he has been pencilled in as a definite entry for the 1976 British Open, but rumour also has it that his female counterpart in the secret training camp, Tatiana Malenkaya, will emerge to joust with the British women golfers before then.

The year 1974 will see the golf boom finally become reality on the continent of Europe. The wealthy and the aristocratic minority of Spain, Portugal and France are at last beginning to realise that their titanic efforts to keep the game out of reach of the majority are akin to those of poor King Canute of yore. But it is Germany's vast and wealthy middle-class that will be the immediate target of the golf-course architects and developers and equipment salesmen in 1974. Having talked for years about building municipal courses, the French will eventually start to do so at last, prompted more by a desire to cash in on the tourist bonanza than a genuine wish to allow their own people to participate in the fastest growing participant sport in Britain and America.

The Spanish professionals have given a lead to those imprisoned in the caddie sheds throughout Europe by emerging as the most powerful phalanx to challenge the hitherto

33

insuperable British. They quickly realised that by turning professional and going on the new, lucrative tour and winning the odd Open Championship in Europe they virtually wrote their own passports of deliverance from the extreme poverty bracket.

Meanwhile in the East the Japanese are emerging as the most likely threat to American world dominance, and it seems only a matter of time – maybe it will come in 1974 – before Masashi "Jumbo" Ozaki annexes his first major title. How fitting it would be if this engaging character could resist the powerful pressures that only just overcame Peter Oosterhuis at Augusta National Golf Club in April. The Masters remains unique because the club reserves the right to invite anyone its members think fit to grace the glorious acres of this former shrub nursery. I fancy there will be a black man in the draw

in the spring of 1974, but I shall be very surprised if he survives the half-way cut, so great will be the emotional and other pressures upon him.

The World Circuit beloved of Peter Thomson – who was the first visionary to make any concrete steps towards its realisation – grows ever nearer to fruition as it becomes more and more expensive to play on the American tour, even if a youngster is good enough to win his card there in perhaps the most difficult competitive event in the world – the U.S.P.G.A. School examination. Ironically at the time of writing the one country apparently dropping out as a source of income for the globe-trotting professional is Australia. But I confidently predict the professional elder statesmen there will stop feuding amongst themselves in 1974, when the tour will finally prosper again, with the

34

PETER THOMSON, *five times winner of the Open Championship, and the first man to attempt to put a world circuit into operation.*

forward-looking Thomson re-creating the tournament circuit he did so much to put together in the first place.

Barry Jaeckel proved by winning the 1972 French Open before failing by a single stroke to win his U.S.P.G.A. card that a good living can be made in pleasant surroundings by the hordes of young, talented, but largely disillusioned Americans willing to try their luck in Europe. Things will become more difficult on Monday mornings in America in 1974, when more and more young players will be competing for fewer and fewer places in the tournament proper. Joe Dey's hopes of a satellite tour to improve on this ridiculous situation – a player must score better to prequalify than he is likely to do in order to win the tournament proper – will finally be shown to be without substance in fact in 1974. Americans are just not interested in

second best. Millions more dollars will be available in the major tournaments during the year, but not for the satellite events the U.S.P.G.A. Commissioner hoped would accommodate the hundreds of golf scholarship boys hoping to cash in on their talent.

I fear that in 1974 more of this latter category, and the continued improvement of the European professionals, will give the British their leanest year to date. The Americans will eventually tear themselves away from their hamburgers and coke to travel Europe on a diet of – yes – hamburgers and coke. And some, like Jaeckel, will become wine drinkers, and learn that life need not begin and end in California.

The year 1974 will finally witness the crumbling of the "Big Three", an expression that originally became redundant on the arrival of Lee Trevino, more so on the departure of Jack Nicklaus from the Mark McCormack stable. Arnold Palmer will finally stop telling attentive pressmen how he should take a rest until he can learn to putt again even half-way decently, and will take it. He will leave competitive golf before sliding sadly any further down its immensely competitive ladder. Gary Player will finally stay at home where his heart, he tells us, belongs, and Jack Nicklaus, having passed Bobby Jones's tally of 13 major championship victories, will start designing the golf courses he tells us are where his heart lies. Palmer will go into politics to fill the gap left by Nixon and Company in the ranks of the Republican Party.

Who will be the new super stars? Lanny Wadkins and Jim Simons – students of Wake Forest University, Palmer's alma mater – are good bets to win more than $100,000 each, the former possibly close to a quarter of a million. That may not be enough to stop Ben Crenshaw, the brilliant young Texan,

35

BARRY JAECKEL *failed to win his American tournament player's card – yet proved himself good enough to win the French Open in 1972. This gives a clear indication of the tremendously high standard of tournament golf at all levels in America.*

from topping the money winners' list. In Britain Peter Oosterhuis will take up Jacklin's mantle as the latter becomes something of a local squire in his adopted Gloucestershire, and in Europe a Garrido or will it be a Gallardo – no, probably Manuel Pinero will emerge as more than a brilliant prospect – a big winner.

At the top level in amateur golf there is a very live danger that the majority of youngsters will start to be frightened away from the game by soaring prices unless the Royal and Ancient Golf Club of St. Andrews and the United States Golf Association relax their incredibly harsh Rules of Amateur Status that are so unrealistic in the modern era. It would be a tragedy if the ranks of amateur golf were once again to become the exclusive preserves of the sons of the wealthy, just when it seemed that anyone good enough

in these islands could gain international recognition at last. But ironically a game that was once dominated by the old-school-tie brigade may be controlled in that way once again.

In America it is the ever-escalating cost of travel and accommodation that is taking its toll on the amateur game, which is why recent Walker Cup teams have contained an unwieldy mixture of largely middle-aged wealth and semi-professional college boys.

Of course there is, and always will be, ever-increasing intensity of competition in amateur golf because of the huge rewards awaiting the even mildly talented in the professional ranks. But those rewards will also ensure a fast turnover amongst amateurs unable to afford the luxury of retaining that status as the cost of living soars so rapidly.

I hope I am proved wrong – just as I was

36

Where is Golf Going in 1974?

Two big winners for the future? LANNY WADKINS *(left) and "Awesome"* JIM JAMIESON. *Both rocketed to prominence in 1972 and have continued to make a big impression on the American circuit. Ben Wright sees them as championship winners in 1974.*

most embarrassingly at St. Andrews in 1971, when only a hasty, well-concealed getaway by fast car saved me from immersion in the Swilcan Burn by the British team – but I see 1974 as a year of re-building for another attempt to win back the Walker Cup on British soil in 1975. Finally the old guard will have to be weeded out, and British amateur golf will not be quite the same without such household names as Michael Bonallack, Rodney Foster, Charlie Green and the like.

By contrast the British professional game can only have gone from strength to strength following victory in the Ryder Cup match at Muirfield, and the stimulus afforded to the game by the battle for supremacy between Jacklin and Oosterhuis. The only trouble will be that these two will dominate the British game because so few rivals of real class will emerge in 1974 – except from the Iberian Peninsula.

Who will win the four major events in 1974? How about Nicklaus at Augusta, Wadkins for the U.S. Open, Oosterhuis for ours and "Awesome" Jim Jamieson, perhaps the best young hopeful from the technical standpoint in America, for the U.S.P.G.A. Championship.

The European Tournament Players' Division will decide at its first meeting of 1974 that while promoters have a perfect right to offer appearance money to Jacklin it can only be in the form of a guarantee. For instance, Jacklin can be offered £2,500 to appear in the Italian Open – again the best endowed in Europe – and if he wins but £500 in prize money the sponsors will then pay him the extra £2,000. But if Jacklin was to win first prize in 1974 of £7,500 he would be paid no appearance money at all.

One ghastly consequence of the golf boom will be that an even greater number of American club golfers will descend on

39

Where is Golf Going in 1974?

Will ARNOLD PALMER *quit golf and move into politics? This tongue-in-cheek prediction could have some basis in fact.*

Europe in 1974 by the jumbo jetful to clog up the courses of southern Spain and Portugal, despite the high rate of golf-course development there. Nowhere in the world in 1974 will the latter be able to keep pace with the former as the average American finally tires of Florida golf in the sun and shirtsleeves, and arrives also in Britain to battle with the elements on our great courses – at least those not already ruined and coarsened by the misuse of automatic watering systems.

There will be the odd fight between British golfers anxious to educate their transatlantic rivals into the intricacies and desirability of match-play rather than medal. But the Americans will largely continue to bring golf almost to a standstill in the resort complexes with their absurd insistence on holing out in however many ill-conceived shots at every one of the 18 holes. Tennis will gain further ground in 1974 in the country clubs of America, who will further feel the chill draught of excessive taxation, as will the conventional golf clubs of Britain. Tennis is winning converts from golf because the five- and six-hour round is now considered normal in America, and wives and families continue to put their feet down. No, Daddy can't slope off to golf at weekends because it takes too damned long – and in any case he comes home half. . . .

There will be every indication in Britain in 1974 that a four-hour round is the norm, a horrifying sign of the times, but at least there will be signs that a great number of new courses are going to be built at last. Unfortunately for those companies that will go to the wall in 1974 and beyond, there will be far too many trying to jump on the golf architecture and construction bandwagon.

On the subject of golf equipment, I predict that 1974 will be a momentous year be-

cause a hurriedly convened meeting of a joint committee set up by the R. & A. and U.S.G.A. will outlaw the carbon graphite shaft and the Uniroyal hexagonal dimple Plus 6 golf ball. It will be decreed that in the interests of the game and its existing courses only the metals and materials in use before the advent of carbon graphite can be used in the manufacture of golf clubs. Golf-ball dimples will have to be round, and they will conform to exact measurements and numbers laid down by the committee. The detachable tungsten weight inserts into iron clubs to achieve heel and toe balance will also be summarily banned, and there will be a great upsurge amongst club golfers of the sales of aluminium clubs that can help them.

The pitch and run shot will grow ever scarcer in 1974 as grasses are coarsened by watering systems, and greens become more and more like the puddings beloved of Americans, who prefer their target golf. But just as surely the continued installation of these irrigation systems will cause a sharp rise in club subscriptions that will snowball. At last British golfers will have to pay a realistic price for their golf. The vast majority of run-of-the-mill golf clubs here will finally be shamed into improving their at present spartan, or plainly inadequate changing rooms, showers, bars and catering to keep pace with members who grow steadily more demanding, and can and will change and shower, eat and drink in comfort elsewhere.

The pattern of the future in club development will swing more towards the residential country-club layout with full leisure facilities for the family, or at the other end of the scale the cut-price course with few niceties that is put together quickly to help in its humble way to satisfy a presently staggering demand that knows no bounds.

The conventional golf club as we have come to know it is quickly going out of fashion.

The millions who fall handily into the bracket of "the backbone of the game" will hopefully hear no more of the compromise 1·66-inch-diameter golf ball in 1974. Hopefully the 1·68-inch variety will become the competitive ball for both amateurs and professionals the world over at national and international level. Certainly the present situation that allows the small ball to be used on the continent of Europe in professional events, when the large one is mandatory in Britain, is one of the game's more ludicrous anomalies which will be put right in 1974.

I believe that the ruling bodies both in America and Britain responsible for pushing the compromise ball will save their faces by shelving it, to avoid a further head-on confrontation with the golf-ball manufacturers, a powerful and united body, particularly in America. But while doing so the R. & A. and U.S.G.A. are perhaps unlikely to agree to opt for the big ball in 1974 – at least until their blushes have faded, and their last feeble protests in favour of the 1·66-inch variety of golf ball have died away to an inaudible murmur.

Hopefully the same two bodies, instead of trying to force something on millions of golfers the latter plainly do not want or need, will try to evolve a more workable and realistic handicapping system for 1974 that will be standardised throughout the world. The present set-up is so loose and open to abuse everywhere that pro-ams are fast becoming laughably corrupt fiestas for an increasing number of golfing bandits.

If handicapping needs reform, nothing in the game is more urgently in need of attention than the vexed Rules of Golf. With a World Circuit now almost complete the need for accurate translation into the various languages involved becomes essential in 1974, if a repetition of the incident at the Italian Open involving Luciano Grappasonni is to be avoided. Poor Grappasonni was penalised two strokes for identifying, rather than merely searching for his plugged ball in a bunker. Such an infringement of the Rules is defined clearly in the authorised English version, but in translation into Italian has become anything but lucid. A major debt will be owed by all of golfing mankind to the man or men able to condense the dreaded Rules into an even remotely explicable form, before they are translated accurately into other languages.

I am convinced that not all continental professional golfers who cheat – did you see that photograph of a Spaniard treading on a small tree to hold it out of his way? – do so intentionally. Unfortunately some of them do, and 1974 could see some angry moves from the British to stamp on those who have shown such proficiency with the leather mashie and other crooked devices. But there is little doubt that the emergent Europeans are going to have to pass through a P.G.A. School where they are taught the Rules if the unintentional contraventions of them are going to be stamped out – as they must be – with so much golf likely to appear on television.

Of course, most of what I have conjectured is wishful thinking, nothing more so than the hope that Oosterhuis will win the British Open. But I shall be surprised if some of the forecasts are not very close to the mark, even hazarded a year ahead of time. We shall see.

Peter Oosterhuis – set to win the Open
Championship at Royal Lytham in 1974?

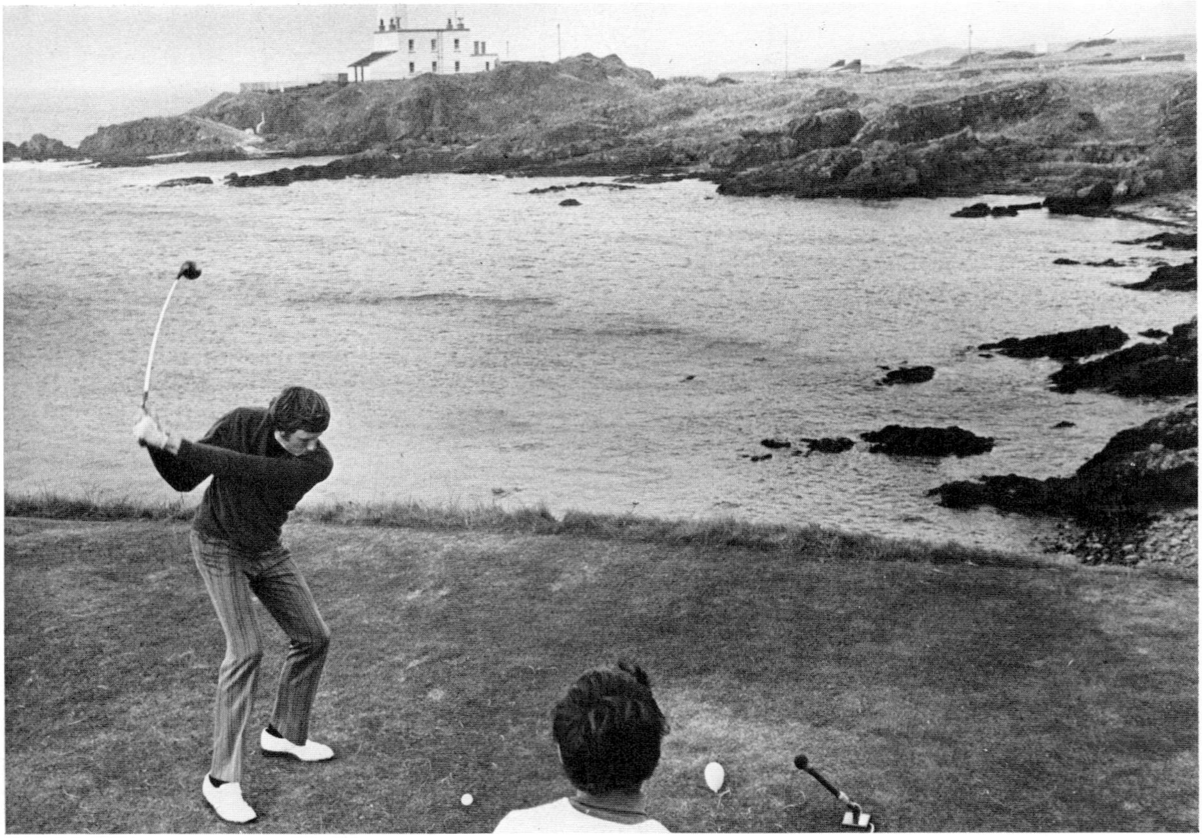

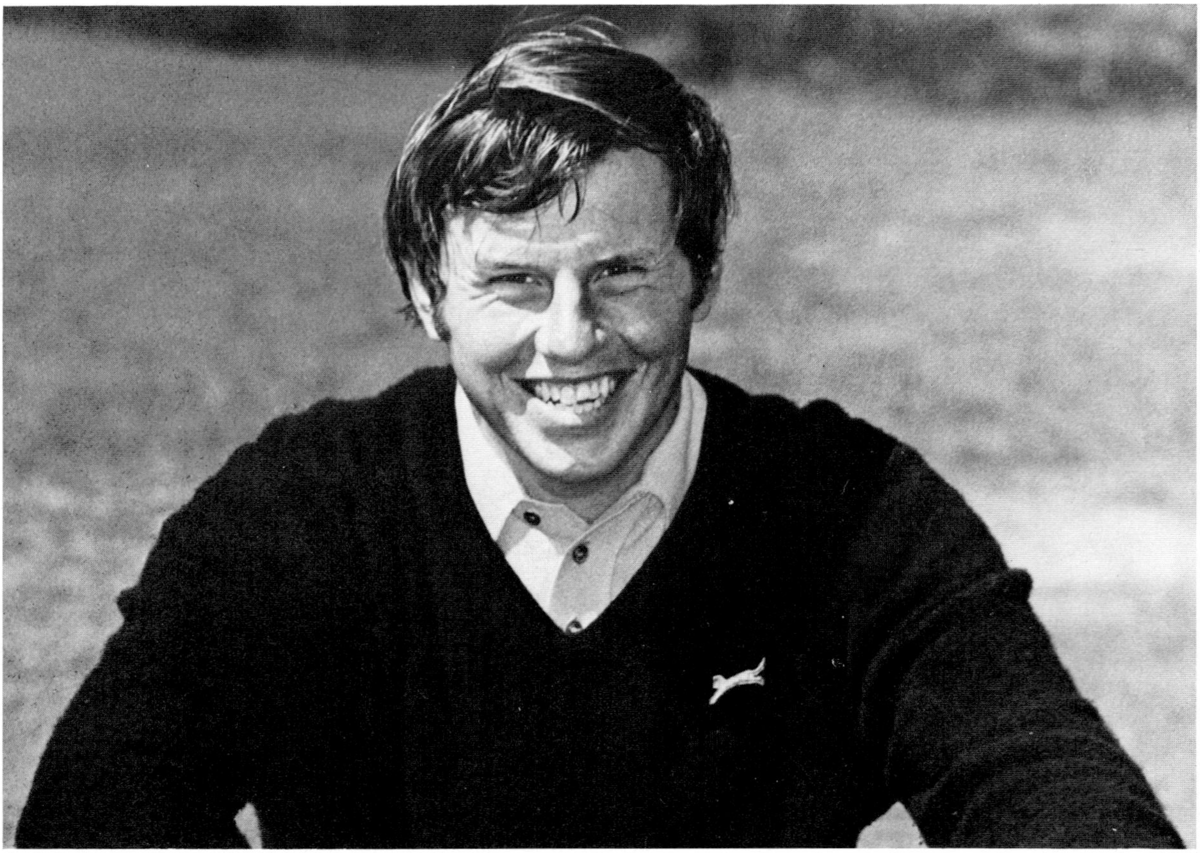

Peter Oosterhuis

"My game used to come apart on the hook side. Because the hook was so destructive I worked hard on eliminating it and now I can carve the thing miles right if I swing too fast."

"I find it helpful to have developed a belief in myself. Every time I tee up I know that I can beat 90 per cent of my rivals comfortably. I know that if I play really well I am the equal of or better than the other 10 per cent."

"I don't consciously try to be on my own, but I do think the 'loner' thing helps. When I play in a group of four I find it difficult to think at all, let alone constructively, about my game or the golf course. I am a bad practice-round player."

"I am convinced that I can learn more from watching certain great players than I can by trying to work things out for myself. I like watching their rhythm, which creates good timing."

"My only ambition is to try to establish myself as a world-class player, and the only way I can do that is by playing in America as well as everywhere else in the world."

"Golf is both a business and a hobby to me, although it is still very much a game that I can enjoy."

5

Life up the Television Tower

by Henry Longhurst

Television has been to me almost the happiest item in a lifelong connection with the game of golf, not least because it so obviously has given so much pleasure to other people. The B.B.C., I gather, have two "ratings", the first being the normal one of how many people watched a given programme; the other, less widely known and I do not even know what it is called, being to what degree those who did watch it liked it. In the latter golf rates very high. Those who do like it like it a lot, some with the almost passionate intensity of a football fan. Those who don't, turn it off.

I have not, of course, the slightest idea how it works and each time it actually does, which nowadays is always, it seems yet another technical miracle. Each time I listen to the hectic preliminary chatter I think to myself: "This time it really isn't going to come right in the end. This time it really is too late." But within seconds of the off there comes a sudden silence and there is Harry Carpenter once again saying: "Welcome to Wentworth. . . ." Golf television is clearly,

In the early days of his life up the television tower HENRY LONGHURST *is seen commentating for the B.B.C. at St. Andrews surrounded by the trappings of his trade.*

even to the layman like myself, much harder to produce than other outdoor games, if only because it is played over a long stretch of country instead of an arena. I sometimes think that even I, given an hour or two's instruction, could produce some sort of programme at, say, Wimbledon, where you have only to plug the cameras into the same spots as last year and watch the players confined to exactly the same court, with someone else doing the scoring for you. In golf they may be stretched over a mile and a half, as they are over the long run-in at Wentworth, which involves the longest stretching of cameras on any television course, though to me it is in many ways the most attractive. Autumn is my favourite time of year and now that we have colour television the scene there with the trees in full glory at the turn of the year can be breathtaking.

Another advantage is that, like the Masters, the Piccadilly tournament is played always on the same course and therefore the regular television customers come to know where they are, so to speak. Though earlier and, to look back upon, somewhat entertaining experiments were made in golf television, it was at Wentworth that the first live tournaments were shown, under the enthusiastic direction of Antony Craxton, who used to take care of the Queen's Christmas

Towers are part of LONGHURST'S *life. Here he stands outside one of the twin windmills which form part of his home on the Sussex Downs.*

broadcasts, and I always remember being told how a surprising number of people were found to enjoy watching a game which many at that time did not understand. "It seemed to be such a lovely place," they said.

I am not asking you to say – "Oh, no!" – when I say that, if things go well, commentators get much more of the credit than they deserve, presumably because they are the only audible link with the programme. The truth is that in an emergency almost anyone reasonably articulate and familiar with the game could do the commentary at a moment's notice, provided it were impressed upon him that he has got to watch the picture on his monitor and not look out of the window. I refer, of course, to golf, not to miracles like Peter O'Sullevan's interpretations of horse races. The real credit should go to the director and producer behind the scenes, in the B.B.C.'s case Slim Wilkinson and Alan Mouncer, who set the whole operation up and conduct the battle, often for hours without a break, from a dark "ops room" concealed somewhere in the bushes.

The commentator, as I have said, gets much of the glory when things go right, though when they don't he has to bear a good deal of "Why ever didn't you show . . . or why ever did you cut us off just when . . .", and no amount of "That part of it is nothing to do with me" will get one away with it.

People, of course, come to recognise your name and, particularly, your voice and it is

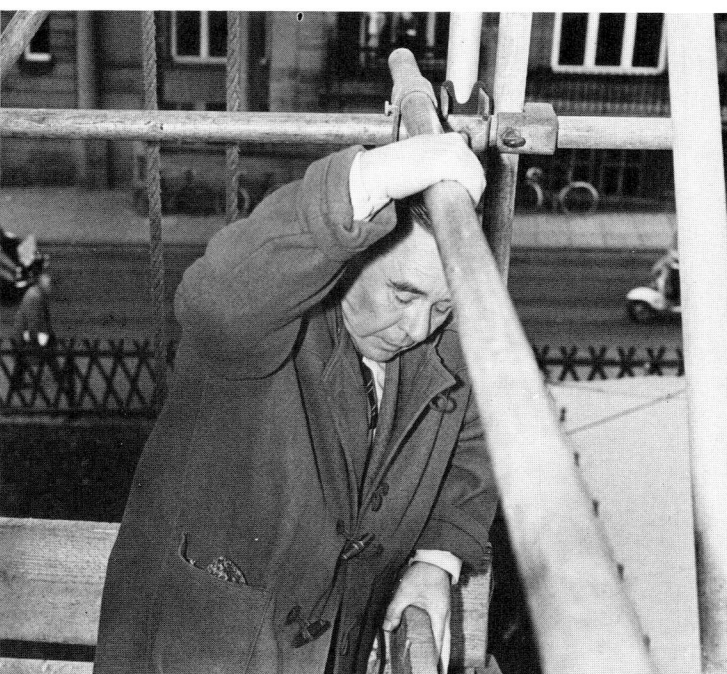

Climbing up to the commentary box and down again can present considerable problems, particularly in bad weather. The crowded operating space does not exactly match up to the glamorous image of life as a television commentator.

51

no use pretending that this does not engender a certain smug satisfaction. It is especially true of London taxi drivers, who actually have a golfing society of their own. One who picked me up at Victoria not only recognised me the moment I opened my mouth but actually insisted on driving me for nothing. I did my honest best to press the fare into his hand but he was so insistent as actually to back his cab away!

The filmed matches "U.S. versus The World", a number of them played at Wentworth, also had the most extraordinary result, as far away even as New Zealand, where in 1970 I was assured that these alone had been responsible for such a golfing "explosion" as to cause the membership of one club to rise from 75 to 500 and a waiting list. The pictures, being black and white off a colour print, were appalling (they are getting colour soon) but everybody – perhaps, be it whispered, because they have only one channel – appeared to have seen them and as I walked down Prince's Street in the essentially Scottish out-post of Dunedin, from which Scott sailed to the Pole, I was not only accosted on all sides with an almost embarrassing friendliness but even hailed by some construction workers on top of a new building. Such is fame!

The only time really when a commentator has to show a certain quickness of wit is when one small voice in the back of the head says:

"Go on! Say it!" and the other says: "No, no. Be careful." Whether you say it or not, the moment is gone in a flash and you are left wishing you had – or hadn't. In a Curtis Cup match at Lindrick, for instance, one of the American girls, a handsome figure of a woman (to give credit where it is due, it was Jo-Anne Gunderson) was to be observed from the rear, bending over in tight red trousers to tee up her ball. I think it must have rolled once or twice off the tee, but at any rate this engaging prospect filled the screen for such time as to be embarrassing. "Go on. Say it," said the small voice. "Say: 'Well, no one can say that the B.B.C. doesn't give both sides of the picture.'" This would have brought a good-natured roar of mirth from hundreds of thousands of people and I kick myself to this day that I let it slip.

Again, during the play-off between Peter Thomson and David Thomas for the Open, some clot – a doctor, too, would you believe it? – actually rang through to London (who in turn rang through to the producer at Lytham, who in turn informed me while we were actually on the air), to say: "Tell Longhurst that there is no 'p' in Thomson." "Go on. Say it. Say: 'Yes, and Thomson isn't the only thing in which the "p" is silent.'" I did not say that either and, though in many ways I wish I had, I suppose I am glad I didn't. But I still have regrets about Miss Gunderson.

6

How to Buy a Better Game

The development of golf equipment

by Geoffrey Cotton

Recent announcements made by practically all golf-equipment manufacturers have been hitting the headlines almost daily. If a club golfer used all the pieces of equipment at one time he might expect to outhit Jack Nicklaus easily – rather like the motorist who found a device that reduced petrol consumption by 25 per cent, fitted four to his car, and expected to run on no petrol at all!

From this it would be reasonable to deduce that all the claims made by manufacturers are exaggerated, but they are not! It is impossible to stop progress, whether it is in the field of medicine, aeronautics or sport. Indeed we are fortunate in that golf clubs and golf balls have been considerably improved in recent years as a result of developments originally made for the aerospace industry.

The most recent innovation, carbon-fibre golf shafts, was evolved after the wonderfibre had been originally developed for use in jet aero engines. In order to reduce the high cost of manufacturing the basic material, the research teams set out to put this special substance to as many uses as possible. Only in this way could carbon fibre itself survive in a world already conditioned to high-cost materials.

Does a carbon-fibre golf shaft really turn a golf club into a magic wand? I don't think so. But, and it is a significant but, I believe it may well improve the total club by up to five per cent, and for a golf club that is quite a big improvement for just one component. The big weight saving, up to 30 per cent, is a real help but there is also the torque characteristic which could help the "touch" golfer to get that bit extra from his swing – rather like the old days of the hickory shaft. The few who managed the "trick" of the "torque" with hickory could hit a golf ball colossal distances. This factor is quite impossible to measure, but all other things being equal, the weight saving allows a golfer to swing the club at a greater speed, thus increasing clubhead speed and assuring more distance.

Another major step forward in golf-club design has been the evolution of the heel-toe weighting principle in iron clubheads. For years leading club makers have been filing and drilling the neck or hosel of an iron, shortening, slimming and lightening this area of the head, whilst at the same time transferring the weight pads out towards the toe to give a better performance. Now, the use of Investment castings has permitted heads to be made to such fine tolerances that scientifically sculptured heads are produced giving the widest sweet spot ever known. For the high-handicap player this is akin to three shots off his handicap at one fell swoop. On top of this, extra heavy tungsten inserts can be placed around the clubhead, at the whim of the designer, to add a little more power to the part that matters.

Wood clubheads have also come in for re-thinking. It all started when Ben Hogan filed a slot in the toe of his woods on the advice of an aerodynamics expert. This was to reduce turbulence behind the head on the downswing. At the time it was considered way-out. Who would have thought, a few years ago, that wings and spoilers would be fitted to racing cars – and work? The new trend in wooden clubhead design is for an extra weight plug to be put either in the toe, or immediately behind the face insert. Logically this could reduce the twisting factor of the clubhead whilst accelerating, and so provide the player with a clubface so nearly at right angles to the line of flight at the moment of impact.

The golf ball has not been left out. The last publicised improvement in my memory was the advent of a saucer-shaped dimple on a ball that was used by my old boss – Richard (Dick) Burton – when he won the British Open in 1939. This was claimed to give a better flight, with more carry. The new hexagonal dimple introduced over 30 years

The drawings below show the gradual development of clubhead design from the days of the hickory shaft to the present larger sweet spot concept.

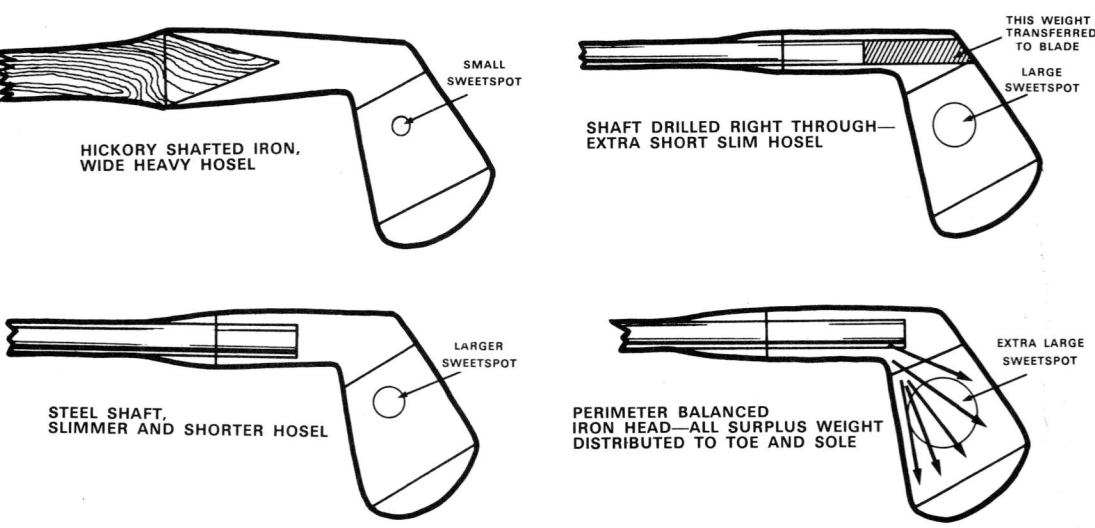

54

The sweet spot on iron clubs is not always the exact geometric centre of the clubface. In fact, in the majority of cases, it lies closer to the heel than the toe of the club. A simple way to detect the centre of your own club's sweet spot is to hold the end of the grip lightly between thumb and forefinger and gently tap the clubface with the point of a pencil. When you tap the centre of the sweet spot the club will rebound straight back without twisting. By chalking the face of your irons on the practice ground you can determine the point where you most frequently make contact with the ball. If this does not coincide with the sweet spot you can make adjustments in the positioning of the clubhead at address.

The pictures here show the exact points on the clubface where golfers of varying handicaps made contact with the ball. In tests carried out by the Acushnet Company in America it was found that low-handicap golfers hit the ball flush on the sweet spot only 41 per cent of the time, while the higher-handicap players achieved this correct contact with only 21 per cent of their shots.

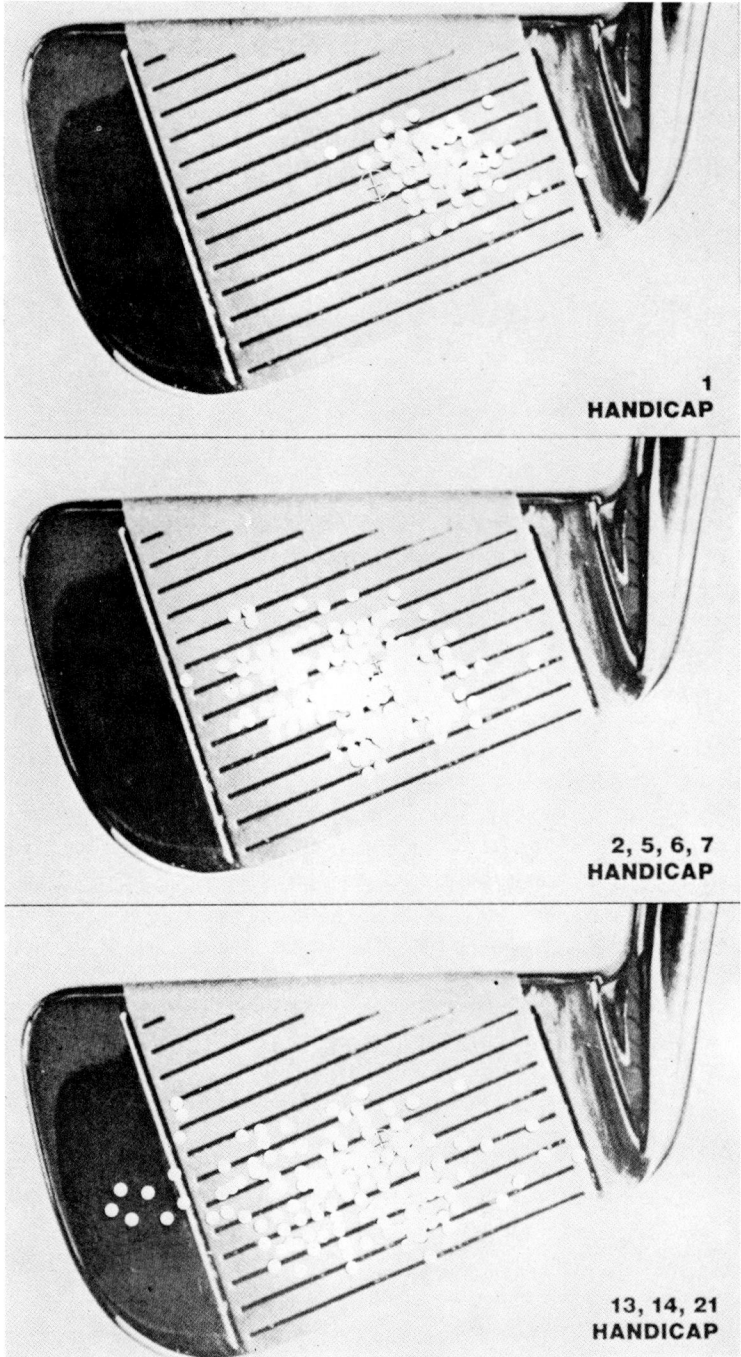

1
HANDICAP

2, 5, 6, 7
HANDICAP

13, 14, 21
HANDICAP

A significant breakaway from traditional golf-
ball design came from the Uniroyal Company
with the introduction of their Plus Six ball in
Britain and America. This new ball features
hexagonal dimples as opposed to the round ones
used by every other major golf-ball manufacturer –
although square dimples were used on some
British golf balls more than 25 years ago.
Another design feature of the Uniroyal ball is
that it contains only 252 dimples compared with
the standard 336. In wind-tunnel tests (shown
here with a conventional ball) Uniroyal claim
that their new ball, with hexagonal dimples
placed in a random pattern, produced more lift.

56

later makes the same claim, but this time is supported by independent wind-tunnel tests. If sales to the club golfer are any indication of success, then it is a winner.

Although given less publicity, the use of Surlyn by some golf-ball makers is surely of great importance to the intermediate club golfer. This plastic, now used for the cover instead of the old-fashioned Balata, has considerably reduced the cutability of a thin covered, top-grade, ball. So, instead of using a cheap ball, which would not cut easily but also flew a shorter distance than the top quality, you can now play the expert's ball and get full distance with extra durability. It also stays whiter longer than the old cover used to, which must be a godsend to the lady golfer who makes a ball last at least six rounds! Already in almost universal use by all the big makers in America, Surlyn will make its presence felt in Britain as a worthwhile step forward in golf-equipment design.

Whether you try just one of the new ideas available to you in the 1973 pro shop or all of them together, I am confident you will agree that you have plenty of scope for improvement in your game. Manufacturers are constantly finding new ways of improving the equipment to help you achieve lower scores. But, as one of my colleagues said when he heard the title of this article: "Everyone can buy a better game from the Pro by just having a lesson!"

Well, if you add a lesson to carbon-fibre shafts, heel-toe weighted irons, impact weighted woods and Surlyn-covered golf balls with hexagonal dimples, it should be possible for even YOU to break 90 on a good day!

"Everyone can buy a better game from the Pro by just having a lesson!"

57

7 You *too* can be a Short

The golfer with an effective short game, the man who can consistently lay those little pitch and chip shots close enough for a single putt, really does have a tremendous advantage.

The tragic thing is that so few people can command a sound short game when it is well within the reach of golfers of any handicap. It is the area of the game where the man who booms the ball 300 yards off the tee is on exactly equal terms with the chap who can never manage more than 180 yards with a driver. For the little shots around the green everyone starts level. It is a department of the game that calls for good judgment and delicacy and which does not give any advantage at all to the power player.

The technique for the pitch and chip shots is simple and I would stress immediately that the most important factor in any short shot is not to make the shot until you have a clear mental picture of how you want the ball to behave in relation to your position. This is the whole crux of the short game, for until you decide how far the ball should fly and how far it must roll you cannot select the right club for the job. One thing which prevents many people from developing a good short game is their illogical use of a favourite club for every chip shot.

By using the wrong club for the particular job in hand a variable factor is immediately introduced into the shot. If a club with too much loft is selected for a little chip from the fringe it will, in some way, have to be de-

58

Game Expert by John Jacobs

Five-times Open champion PETER THOMSON *demonstrates the fine points of the pitch shot. Full, early wrist-break leading to a sharp downward blow into the back of the ball and flowing into an easy follow-through.*

lofted during the execution of the shot. On the other hand, if the choice of club is too straight-faced there will be an effort to scoop the ball to get it into the air. Selection of the correct club will allow you to play the same, simple shot in any circumstances with the club doing the job for which it is designed and with no variable factors being introduced into the technique of the shot.

Watch the care with which the pros think out these little shots in tournaments and you will get some idea of how important the correct choice of club can be. They work out the spot on which they plan to pitch the ball and how far it should run. When this is decided they take the club which is best suited to the exact task.

Let us get clear in our minds right at the outset the two basic shots which are the foundation of a good short game. A chip is usually played with a fairly straight-faced club (but not always) and has the ball in the air for the minimum amount of time and rolling on the ground for the greater part of the distance it has to cover. A pitch is played with the more lofted clubs and is exactly the opposite, flying the ball for the greater part of its travel and rolling very little once it touches the ground. And, of course, the pitch-and-run is the compromise shot in between the two.

The pitch

There is an enormous fallacy about the pitch

60

shot which many club golfers fall into. They play all these shots as cut-up shots. This means coming into the ball from the outside and blocking the face of the club open at impact. It is a very good and useful shot in difficult circumstances when a high flight trajectory is used to stop the ball virtually in its own pitch mark, but it is not an easy shot to play and requires considerable finesse.

So many people are trying to play every pitch shot this way and turning what can be a relatively simple shot into a difficult one. There is a mistaken belief that the only way to stop a golf ball quickly is to cut it. This just is not true. As I have said, the cut-up shot can be a very useful one, but watch any of the world's great wedge players and you will see

them draw the ball into the pin slightly from right to left and still make it come back off the second bounce – this is achieved much more through backspin as opposed to trajectory. You get plenty of backspin in these short shots simply by hitting down into the back of the ball with a lofted club.

Having said this, it is all too easy for other players to fall into the trap of believing that backspin is the only factor which will stop a golf ball. It is certainly one of the major considerations, but the flight and trajectory of the ball, the position from which the ball is struck (either above or below the level of the green) and the condition of the turf are all points to be considered.

As in all golf shots the correct set-up to the

61

ball is of vital importance. Keep the feet fairly close together in a narrow stance and position the ball mid-way between the feet. A slightly open stance with the feet will help restrict the backswing and will keep the body out of the way to allow the arms to go through to the target. When setting up to the shot with an open stance don't fall into the common error of letting the shoulders follow the line of the feet. Although the stance can be slightly open the shoulders should still remain parallel to the line through the ball

to the target. If the ball is addressed with the feet and shoulders in a open position the player will be set up left of his target and will be forced to hold the blade of the club open at impact to get the ball travelling in the right direction. Having to block the shot at impact in this way makes it very difficult to judge distance – a most important factor with these shots.

Set yourself comfortably over the ball as if sitting on a high stool – flex the knees but don't bend too far over the ball. I would

stress again, don't let the shoulders get too open as this is the main reason for so many wedge shots finishing left of the flag. This out-to-in shoulder position is also the main reason for a flat swing with these short shots from where it is so easy to shank. A correct foot and shoulder set-up gives the feeling of moving the club up slightly inside the line that runs through the ball to the target in the backswing. Start with a quick break of the wrists. From this position the angle of attack into the ball is steep and the line of the swing

JOHN JACOBS *shows the basic similarities between the pitch and chip shots – narrow stance, feet pointing slightly left of target to allow the arms a clear swing-path through to the target, yet the shoulders remaining square to the target line. The main difference between the two shots is that where the pitch shot calls for a full wrist-break and a steep descent of the clubhead into the ball, the chip shot is basically an arm swing, with no conscious use of the hands. Equal length of backswing and follow-through are a good guide to the judgment of distance.*

is from just inside to straight through at impact.

With a lofted club the position of the blade at impact is not quite as important as it is with a driver, or other straight-faced clubs, because contact is made close to the bottom of the ball and a great amount of backspin is imparted. This backspin tends to override the effects of side-spin on the ball and if the face of the club is slightly open at impact there will be little apparent slice spin. It is possible, however, to get a little hook action on the ball from inside to straight through and you will often see a wedge shot hit by a professional curling very slightly from right to left and still stopping very quickly once the ball hits the green. By allowing the hands a free rein, as it were, in the hitting area it becomes much easier to judge the strength and distance of the shot as opposed to the same judgment when the club blade is held open and the ball is cut up.

The chip
The technique for the chip shot is exactly the same as for the pitch, but with one vital difference – there must be no conscious wrist-break on the backswing since we are not trying to hit down and impart backspin. From the same set-up the clubhead is taken back in an identical path initially straight and then inside the line to the target and comes back to the ball from this position to straight through. In fact every golf shot calls for this same swing-path, even a putt – other than the very short ones.

Yet, whereas the pitch shot necessitated a full break of the wrists in the backswing, the chip shot is more of an arm action – although the wrists should be free and not held rigidly firm. Assuming one has a good lie the chip shot is a firm, controlled sweep with the arms and club working together and a little free-

dom in the hips and wrists to go with the shot.

At address the hands should be in front of the clubhead and this relationship should be maintained throughout the swing – the hands always leading the clubhead at impact. This situation would be exaggerated if the ball were lying down in not too good a lie.

With all shots less than full ones we have a further dimension to control – how far shall we swing? Some of these shots are missed from a long backswing and a deceleration in the hitting area while other players do not allow the club to go back far enough for the distance required and therefore develop a quick jab for a downswing. We are looking for a length of backswing from which a smooth acceleration will give us the required distance.

A little practice will tell you how far back to take the club for any length of shot and from that moment concentrate on making a smooth take-away and then accelerating smoothly into and through the ball.

One point I would stress again in summing up the short game is the path of the swing. This, of course, applies to every shot in golf, but is often more noticeable in the little shots. Although the club is taken straight back from the ball initially, it soon must go inside if we are going to get a straight-through blow to the target. The correct swing-path moves initially straight back from the ball then goes inside the line to the target on the backswing and in the downswing comes from inside the line, to straight through at impact and then inside the line again on the follow-through. Since the follow-through is often curtailed with the short shots, from inside to straight through is a good way of thinking of the swing-path.

Never forget that it is within the capabilities of every golfer to be a short game expert.

64

Arnold Palmer, who has now resorted to the wearing of glasses in an attempt to overcome the loss of putting form which has curtailed his achievements in recent years, is still the folk hero of the modern golf game.

Neil Coles, voted this year as Europe's best professional golfer by his tournament opponents, has established a record of remarkable consistency in more than 10 years as a leading money-winner.

Tony Jacklin, first British winner of the Open Championship for 18 years, also captured the American Open title within a year and carried British golf into the 1970s with a flourish.

After a fantastically successful career spanning almost 20 years Christy O'Connor senior shows no signs of handing over the reins to his young nephew, Christy junior.

Miller Barber, better known in America by his nickname of "Mr. X" because he habitually wears dark glasses, has one of the most impossible-looking swings in modern golf. Yet he is a regular money-winner.

Paired together in the Open Championship at Muirfield, Grand Slam bidder Jack Nicklaus and powerful young South African pro Dale Hayes, reach the 18th green amid a blaze of colour.

At an age when most golf professionals have given up competitive play, Sam Snead is still winning tournaments. The natural swing which first won him the U.S.P.G.A. title in 1942 has notched up 131 victories in the intervening years. Now, at the age of 61, he is still able to maintain his position in the top 60 money-winners on the American circuit.

8

The Ryder Cup Story

by Geoffrey Cousins

International contests of various kinds proliferate in the modern golf calendar, and it seems strange to reflect that 50 years ago there was scarcely anything of the kind. The England v. Scotland amateurs' match started in 1902 and the professionals of those two countries followed suit in 1903; and that was all till after the First World War, which perhaps helped to extend the rivalry of nations to the golf links. Mr. G. H. Walker, an American enthusiast, set the ball rolling by presenting a trophy for matches between the amateurs of Britain and the United States, and the first match was played on National Links, Long Island, in 1922. Mr Walker's gesture was probably inspired by an unofficial match at Hoylake in 1921, when the American amateurs won 9–3. The inspiration for the Ryder Cup also came from an unofficial match, played at Wentworth in 1926 and watched by Mr. Samuel Ryder, a St. Albans seed and herb merchant who had recently engaged Abe Mitchell, one of the greatest players of his time, as private coach. Enthusing over Britain's win by 12 points, Mr. Ryder readily fell in with a P.G.A. suggestion of a regular series of matches, and donated the gold cup which bears his name.

When the American professionals played at Wentworth they had only just landed in Britain after a sea voyage and had their sights on the Open Championship four weeks later, which partly explains their heavy defeat. But in 1927, when the chips were down at Worcester, Massachusetts, it was a different story. The Americans, led by Walter Hagen, won $9\frac{1}{2}$–$2\frac{1}{2}$ to become first holders of the trophy. Only two members of the British team, Ted Ray and George Duncan, had been in the United States before, and the absence of Abe Mitchell, who had been taken ill on the boat train to Southampton, was a serious loss.

Duncan, the only British singles winner at Worcester, was appointed captain for the 1929 match at Moortown, Leeds, and in cold, windy weather (there was a snowfall before the match) Britain won 7–5. This occasion saw the debut of Henry Cotton, only 22 but only five years short of being Open Champion. He celebrated international rank by beating Al Watrous 4 and 3, and Duncan had the great satisfaction of beating Hagen 10 and 8 in the captains' match.

If the cold weather had affected the Americans at Moortown, it was heat that beat Britain two years later at Columbus, Ohio. The Mid-West sweltered in a heatwave which created humid, enervating conditions, and the Americans, better acclimatised, won comfortably by nine matches to three. The British were also weakened by the

73

The Ryder Cup Story

For the first time in the history of the event, the Ryder Cup matches between Britain and America were halved at Royal Birkdale in 1969. Britain's captain ERIC BROWN *gets a tentative grip on the gold trophy as America's captain* SAM SNEAD *holds it aloft.*

absence of three leading players. Cotton, who had objected to the conditions – all earnings on the trip to be pooled and everyone to go and return as a team – declined to take part; and Percy Alliss and Aubrey Boomber, who held appointments in Berlin and Paris respectively, were ineligible because they were not domiciled in Britain.

In 1933 the Cup returned to British hands in a very exciting way. After a long and close contest in the singles, watched by 15,000 people and followed with interest by the Prince of Wales, everything depended on how Syd Easterbrook and Densmore Shute played the last hole on the Southport and Ainsdale links. They stood on the 18th tee all square, and teams were level, too, at five and a half points each. Both drives were bunkered, both players took three to reach the green, and each had a longish putt for the par figure. Easterbrook putted first and ran his ball stone dead. Shute's putt was downhill on a green made slippery by the day's play, and his ball ran four feet past the hole. He missed the one back and Britain had won by a single point.

This result continued the pattern of alternative home wins but after regaining the cup at Ridgwood New Jersey in 1935 the Americans made no mistake on their second visit to Southport, winning 8–4, despite the return of Cotton, who beat Tony Manero, and the successful debut of Dai Rees, who beat Byron Nelson, then America's No. 1 golfer, by 3 and 1.

The 1939 match, due to be played at Jacksonville with Cotton as captain, was cancelled owing to the war, and it would have been better for British morale if the revival, in 1947, had been still further delayed. The world had just emerged from a terrible, exhausting period and our players, after five years of rationing and no com-

petitive golf, were in no way ready for a major international contest. Furthermore the P.G.A. hadn't the funds to finance a trip to America. Fortunately, or unfortunately, according to the point of view, a wealthy wholesale grocer in Oregon, Bob Hudson, cast himself in the role of fairy godfather. He arranged for the match to be played on the Portland club's course in November, and made himself responsible for the cost. The weather for the match was wet and miserable, as might be expected in a northern State at that time of the year, but the British, so far from profiting by familiar conditions, were outplayed from start to finish, losing all the foursomes and being saved from a whitewash by Sam King beating Herman Keiser in the last single.

That was the nadir of Britain's Ryder Cup fortunes and we can trace from that defeat a steady revival through the near misses of Ganton in 1949 and Wentworth in 1953 to the amazing triumph at Lindrick in 1957. Ganton will always be remembered for two things – the sight of Ben Hogan, non-playing American captain, hobbling about in the slow stages of recovery from a car accident which everyone thought had ended his career; and the avalanche of birdies and eagles which swept away British hopes after the home side had led 3–1 in the foursomes. Hogan, thin-lipped, uncompromising and seething with the fury of enforced inaction, pep-talked his men that evening, and on the morrow they went on a riotous orgy of brilliant figures. The eight British players in the singles finished altogether 34 under fours for the day. But the Americans were 56 under fours, and won the singles 6–2 to take the match 7–5.

At Wentworth, with Henry Cotton as captain, the fortunes swayed backwards and forwards through two thrilling days. Britain's

74

team included three newcomers – Eric Brown, already seasoned, and two youngsters, Peter Alliss, 22, and Bernard Hunt, 23. America won the foursomes 3–1 and although we fought well in the singles it looked all over when Weetman was five down with six to play against the redoubtable Sam Snead. But Snead went off his driving – fatal over the West Course finish – and Weetman won the remaining six holes to snatch a victory. Again hope gleamed and all depended on the youngsters. If Alliss could win the last hole and halve with Joe Turnesa and if Hunt could halve the last hole and beat Dave Douglas, the cup would be ours. Those "ifs". With all the world watching, the strain was too much. Alliss lost and Hunt only halved his match, and America scrambled home by a single point.

Four years later Dai Rees had the tremendous thrill of leading Britain to the first post-war victory, just 20 years after he had been on the losing side in America's first win in Britain. Lindrick was the highspot of Ryder Cup history for Britain, the more so because victory came out of the blue after we had lost the foursomes 1–3. From the very start of the singles the Americans seemed to be out of gear, and Rees's men, pressing home the advantage and cheered on by crowds who grew more and more enthusiastic as the great day moved to its climax, won the singles 6–1 and the match by three points. It was, as Bob Hudson said after witnessing this triumph, "a shot in the arm for British golf".

In the meantime all the contests on American soil had been won by the home players, and Britain duly lost the Cup in 1959

75

The picture that says it all. TONY JACKLIN *and* JACK NICKLAUS *halve the final match to give Britain and America an equal share of the Ryder Cup in 1969.*

in California. Several of the 36-hole matches finished way out on the course and this suited neither the spectators nor the television cameras. Hence the decision to play the 1961 match at Lytham-St. Annes by 18-hole games. This meant that America's usual 3–1 foursomes lead became 6–2 on the opening day and when the visitors won five of the eight points in the first series of singles, interest evaporated. In 1963 the match took the present form, being extended to three days with the foursomes and singles sandwiching two series of 18-hole four-ball matches. Result: America 23, Britain 9.

The match moved for the first time to Birkdale in 1965 with Harry Weetman as captain, and with the novel trappings of a full-scale "tented village". It was a close contest in the sense that, although the Americans won by seven points, everything depended on some close finishes in which putts missed or holed made all the difference. Unfortunately, true to form, the Americans did most of the holing and we did most of the missing.

After a 1967 defeat at Houston, Texas a young British team, which included Tony Jacklin, Maurice Bembridge and Peter Townsend, went very near to victory at Birkdale in an exciting contest which saw the home players start the afternoon singles with a lead of two points, thanks partly to a 4 and 3 win for Jacklin over the redoubtable Jack Nicklaus. Young Gallacher also distinguished himself on that thrilling afternoon by beating Lee Trevino, but from that moment the tide ran against Britain. Both Brian Huggett and Jacklin made great efforts against Billy Casper and Nicklaus respectively, and although they gained honourable halves the victory which would have given Britain the Cup eluded both. So it was a tie, the first in the history of the event, and America kept the Cup.

For several years now it had been obvious that British golfers were becoming much more accustomed to golf in America and the 1971 contest at St. Louis, Missouri, was very close. Five games were halved, and of the others the Americans won 16 against 11, but that advantage was due only to the fact that they gained six and a half points from the eight four-ball games. On the traditional foursomes and the familiar singles the British players held their own, which encouraged the hope that some day, not far distant, a British victory in the United States would add one more page to the history of the Ryder Cup.

77

Lee Trevino

"Who can dare say I have a bad swing? The only thing that matters in golf is the score you put on the board. You don't have to look pretty out there, you have to win. Look at my record and tell me who has a better swing than mine."

"When you are playing for five bucks and you've got two bucks in your pocket — that's pressure. Where's the pressure when you've got a five-footer for the Open? Hole it or miss it you still wind up with a pocket full of dollars."

"An extended take-away and full follow-through, together with firm control of the club through the hands, are essential for successful long-iron play."

79

"It would be against the law of averages for one man to win three Open championships in the space of 24 days — but I've been beating the law of averages all my life."

"Nobody can play square-to-square if they set-up with their feet and hips square to the ball. Setting-up that way means that you have to swing round yourself. I'm the only guy in the world that swings square-to-square because I get my feet and hips out of the way at address and give myself room to swing the clubhead along the line to the hole for a greater distance. Nobody has a longer extension with the right arm and right shoulder through the ball than me."

10

Play-Slow Flo by Dan Jenkins

Where I came from, a so-called lady golfer was always something to be hollered at, like an overheating '53 Buick blocking traffic, or a sullen waitress who couldn't remember to put cheese on the 'burger and leave off the onions, the dummy. Hey, you. You up there on the green with the legs like tree bark, and the schoolteacher skirt and the one-foot putt. It's *good*. I give you the putt, all right? So take your 135 shots back to the mixed grill and jump into your vodka martini with your nitwit husband who took your father's thieving money and built the country club and won't let you play here but once a week – in front of *me*. Go shell some peas or crochet an afghan or do whatever women ought to be doing instead of cluttering up a golf course. Fore!

That's how it was growing up back in Texas. The most fun was to stand back there with your guys and then, after all the yelling and waiting, everybody would cut loose with a three-iron. And then when the shots would burn into the green and go between the putting stances of Slow-Play Fay and Play-Slow Flo, and when they would hop around like an assortment of Ruby Keelers' we'd sink to our knees in aching laughter.

We had it all worked out in our minds that we belonged on the course and they didn't. We were there to sharpen up for the Goat Hills Invitation and they – the women – were there to keep us from becoming the future Hogans. "Women golfers are meece," we said, referring to our plural of moose.

We never asked to play through. We just

did it, often while they were studying their chip shots. And there would always be one of them, a slightly rotund, menacing, scowling soul who would challenge us. "Don't you boys know anything about manners?" she would say.

We would all very wittily ask each other if we knew anything about manners and, while we putted out, we would discuss it. One of us would say he thought he used to know something about manners, back when manners lived over the way. Manners was pretty good, we would say, but he had a tendency to snap-hook it when he got tense. We would be going on towards the next tee and the big lady would still be after us. "I know who you are, and I'm going to tell your parents," she would say.

One of us would say, "That's gonna be a lot of phone calls because we all come from broken homes."

The big lady would usually turn out to be somebody I'll call Mrs. R. F. Zinger, 14 times city champion and president of the women's district golf association. She would be the first lady ever to pass the local bar exam, the first lady pilot, a former Curtis Cup girl, an ex-national spelling champion, the daughter of the city's first four-term mayor, the author of a textbook on the history of the Colorado River and the architect of the town's new motorway system.

With Mrs. R. F. Zinger lecturing after us, we would bound off down the fairway, having successfully played through, but of course a couple of us would insist on calling something back at her from out of slung-wedge distance.

Such was my fondness for women's golf in those days. Not to suggest, however, that my attitude would be changed by a certain maturity or my advancement into newspaper work. Anyone who ever did time on a newspaper sports desk is familiar with the type of phone calls you get from lady golfers. Mine usually came when I was listening to the Kentucky Derby and the horses were at the post. I would get the call from Mrs. Simcox reporting the net 77 that Mrs. Slocum shot to win the local women's golf association's Tuesday Flag Tournament.

"I'm *sure* it was a net 77," Mrs. Simcox would say. "Let's see. She bogeyed 1, double-bogeyed 2. . . ."

Yeah, yeah, yeah.

I guess my most favourite phone call of all time – true story – went something like this:

Me: Hi, sports fans. Pegler here. Runyon's out to lunch.

"Sports department, please."

This here's it.

"Is this the sports department?"

Take it on one, Hildy.

"Hello? Sports department?"

Hi!

"This is Mrs. J. D. Stephens calling for Mrs. R. F. Zinger, the president of the women's district golf association. Mrs Zinger asked me to call you because she said you always wanted the results of our weekly tournaments."

Oh, good.

"Mrs. Zinger said you liked to print the results."

Well, Mrs. Zinger looks out for us pretty good.

"Mrs. Zinger said to tell you that we played our weekly blind-flag bogey event today, and I have the results."

You played a what?

"Our weekly blind-flag bogey tournament is what Mrs. Zinger called it."

What exactly is that?

"Well, it was sort of complicated, but we all played and I have the winners here."

Fine. What was it again?

84

"It was our weekly blind-flag bogey tournament, a different type of event that Mrs. Zinger thought up."

O.K.

"I'm not sure I can explain it, but we all played 18 holes and then Mrs Zinger figured out who won."

O.K. Just start with the winner.

"Well, first place in the championship flight was Mrs. R. F. Zinger. . . ."

It was inevitably my experience that women didn't actually *play* golf. They casseroled it. They all stood there in front of my gangsome, poling at two-inch putts. They all had woefully slow, four-piece backswings with curious hip moves. They took the clubs back so far that the shafts whipped them on the shoulder blades, and then they lunged forward and the clubheads plundered into the earth and the balls went dribbling off into the weeds.

A lot of the time I figured it was the way they dressed that made them play so badly. And slowly. They all wore those goofy things on their feet that weren't socks and came up just above the shoe tops and reached down below the anklebones. Ugly. And they wore straight skirts that hit them below the knees, with white blouses that were too tight, and big-brimmed hats with red bows.

Then there was the cackling in the clubhouse. After their rounds, I noticed that most women golfers could get into the booze better than most men. Several times I thought I saw two women having a bitter fight across a table, but they were just chatting over their Manhattans – or whatever women drink – about curtains and drapes.

I understand, of course, that there were supposed to be a lot of women golfers in the world who weren't like the ones I had always been exposed to. I knew about the lady pros. I knew they had a tour of their own, but I also knew what most guys felt about it: you would have bet that every one of 'em out there on the women's pro tour could overhaul a diesel truck if she put her mind and energy to it.

In recent years I have been presented with a number of chances to visit a women's pro tournament instead of hanging around the men's tour all the time. Each time I gingerly managed to escape, and the assignment most often fell to an associate in the golf department, a child star who writes too well for any of us to loaf much.

"You ought to go see 'em," he would say. "They're great."

Wrong. Got to stay with the guys, I would insist. Tom Weiskopf is getting ready to issue his first quote of the year, and I don't want to miss it.

"It isn't like you remember it," my colleague would argue. "Most of them are cute and friendly, and they can play like hell."

Well, one of these days, I would say. Can't now, though. Got a biggie coming up in Pensacola. Eichelberger's moving up on the points list. McGee's ready to bust out. Crampton smiled the other day. All very exciting with the men.

To be candid about it, one of the things that kept me away from the L.P.G.A. tour was the knowledge that the girls don't exactly travel the caviar circuit in terms of towns.

Also, the names of their tournaments were troubling. They all sounded like stockcar races. For example, there were things like the Shreveport Kiwanis Invitational, the Johnny Londoff Chevrolet, the Len Immke Buick, the Springfield Jaycee and the Lincoln-Mercury.

Then it happened. My young associate said early last spring he thought there might be a women's event coming up that I'd like. The $50,000 Sealy-L.P.G.A. Classic. Sealy makes mattresses.

That's *funny*, I said.

"No, seriously," he said. The men's tour was quiet, after all. Terry Dill wouldn't be changing his grip for another week or so. Dick Lotz still had the same putter. Bert Yancy had postponed his annual interview till July.

"And it's in Las Vegas," he said.

That was the magic word. Vegas. Now, I know that to some people Las Vegas is not all that fascinating. To some, it's Baghdad-in-the-desert, the mob's idea of chic, a neon-lit asylum, the blonde-wig, no-bra, no-brain capital of the Western world. To others, such as me, however, Vegas comes up as the only civilised city in the U.S., because it's the only one where there aren't a lot of lightweight lawmakers trying to tell you that you can't eat, drink, gamble or fall in love between two a.m. and noon. So I take Vegas whenever I can get it, even if I have to fool around with women's golf.

Judging from the number of blue Sealy blazers around The Desert Inn during one full week last May, there weren't many mattresses being sold anywhere. Sealy was venturing into golf for the first time, and the company had selected a women's tournament to sponsor for what it believed to be a tidy statistical reason. Women make or influence nine out of every 10 mattress purchases, said a Sealy press release.

It didn't take long, in Vegas, for me to realise that one of the major differences between lady pros and men pros is that lady pros scream a whole lot more at a dice table. On the first night in town I was trying to have a quiet drink in the lobby bar at The Desert Inn with my old friend Bud Erickson, a

former employee of the Detroit Lions and Atlanta Falcons who had been cast into the unlikely role of executive director of the L.P.G.A., when we heard these female noises ringing through the casino.

"I think those are my people," Bud said.

We looked and there they were, nine of them, jammed around a dice table as if it were a washrag sale. One of them – Gerda Boykin, her name was – was shooting, and she had just rolled a seven. Almost everything in The Desert Inn stopped for the next few moments as Gerda Boykin, an attractive brunette who was once the only lady pro in Germany, made three more passes with the dice amid a chorus of some of the best shrieks since Arnie first hitched up his trousers.

What had happened was, a bunch of the girls, including Judy Rankin and Pam Higgins and this Gerda, had formed a syndicate on the tour a few weeks before Vegas. Every time one of them three-putted in a tournament, she put $1 into a pool, and they had this pact that they would take the money to Vegas for the Sealy. And on the first night there, one of them – it turned out to be Gerda Boykin – would shoot the bundle at

craps for three, maybe four rolls. They went in with $60 total, and the nine of them came out with an average of $40 after Gerda got through.

Bud Erickson said, "Pretty good story, huh, right off the bat? Nothing like that on the men's tour, I guess."

Right, I said. You can't find nine guys who'll speak to each other.

"Lot of good stories out here," said Bud. "There's a girl named Diane Patterson who used to be a trapeze artist. She took up golf after she quit The Flying Viennas."

Really?

"Got a kid named Pam Barnett who throws her wig around when she gets mad, instead of breaking clubs."

Good.

"How about the Watusi Kid? Donna Caponi. She'll dance all night and play great golf."

Hmmmmm.

"Got a couple of Japanese girls on the tour now. Chako Higuchi and Marbo Sasaki."

Ah, so.

"Hey," said Bud. "How about Sharron Moran? She's really attractive and she does these hat tricks. She's always wearing a different hat on the course. She must have 20 or more different hats."

Z-z-z-z-z-z-z. Oh, excuse me, Bud. Almost dropped off there for a minute.

The Sealy-L.P.G.A. Classic had an odd format. It was a 72-hole tournament for the girls, of course, with a hefty $10,000 going to the winner. Well, that's big for the women. It's a shrug for the guys. Anyhow, John Montgomery, the tournament director, had it all worked out that to make it different – to give it something extra – it would be played sort of like the Crosby in reverse. The lady pros would have *men* partners every day in what constituted four separate Pro-Ams. In other words, each day the girls would play for some extra cash, and the amateur men would compete for what appeared to be just about all of the Steuben crystal that had ever been sculpted.

On Wednesday evening John Montgomery ran down the list of all the glittering male types from sports and show biz who had been invited to participate. There were Joe Namath, Glen Campbell, Mickey Mantle, Joe DiMaggio, Dale Robertson, Joe Louis, Vic Damone.

"And you," he said.

87

I said uh-duh-*who?*

"You play at 8.42 a.m. with Donna Caponi and Glen Campbell," John said.

Later that evening my lovely wife, whom I shall call June, and I were trying to decide where to go in Vegas – I was torn between *Vive Les Girls* at the Dunes and *Geisha'rella* at the Thunderbird – when she asked what I was going to wear tomorrow morning because there would be a gallery.

The usual, I said. My basic-blue button-down with the sleeves cut off and bush jeans. Maybe the grey sweater.

"You'll smother to death and look stupid," she said. "How's your game?"

Terrific, if I don't shank, I said.

"Then *don't* shank," she said. "What'll Glen and Donna think?"

Relax, I said. What do show-biz guys know about golf? And forget Donna. This is hardly the Masters, you know.

You could probably say that the crowd was fairly large around the first tee, most of them there to see Glay-yun. We stood around for a little bit, posed for pictures and waited for the P.A. to announce our pairing. Donna Caponi came over and said: "You and Glen both have eight strokes. We've got a chance to win this today. We'll just play loose and see what happens."

I told Donna that the tournament itself was the most important thing, where she was concerned. We'd try not to bother her, me and Glen, I said.

"Listen, we're going to have fun," she smiled.

Donna teed off first and whipped it about 240 down the middle with a pretty solid swing, and it suddenly dawned on me that she was, after all, the U.S. Women's Open champion of the past two years.

Glen Campbell stepped up next and flogged it about 260 down the middle with a very good swing, and I wondered where in the hell *that* came from.

I don't recall a great deal of applause when I was announced on the tee, but I do remember teeing up the ball, backing away for a practice swing and seeing my wife over behind the ropes. She was trying to tell me something in a whisper, hoping I could read her lips. Which I could. She was saying: "Take . . . off . . . the . . . dumb . . . sweater. . . . Dummy."

That didn't bother me, however. I opened up with the tee shot I always open up with – a howling slice which, when last charted, was headed so far out of bounds that Glen Campbell said: "Fore on The Strip."

The provisional drive I hit was the same old second effort, a boring hook that hammered its way into the nearest fairway bunker.

"That completes our clinic, folks," Campbell said. And we were off.

It wasn't the most comfortable triple-bogey eight I've ever made because, by notable contrast, Campbell put a spoon up near the green in two and had a couple of leisurely putts for a birdie. Donna raced over and kissed him.

Look, I'm just one, I said. Can I play through?

"If you're not going to *try*," my lovely wife said, "then I'll just go on back to the hotel and wait for you by the swimming pool."

By the end of the third hole I had cost our team a net birdie by missing a two-foot putt – specifically, my wife said, because I refused to take a cigarette out of my mouth before I stroked the ball, and I had smashed another drive out of bounds and made a double bogey.

"You have a good swing," Donna Caponi was kind enough to say, "if you'll slow it down about four speeds."

Yeah, I know what to *do*, I said. It's just that sometimes, if you drink a little. . . .

"You'll be O.K.," Donna said. "Just take it back low and slow."

A little later my lovely wife came over and said, "Can I go get anybody a Coke, or a *golf shirt*, perhaps?"

Billy Casper frequently plays in a sweater in warm weather, I pointed out, rather testily.

"You're soaked under that thing," she said. "Yuk."

I'll tell you what else is making me hot, I said.

There were those in the gallery who, were they willing, could testify that for the next several holes everybody in our threesome, including the dummy, played pretty well. Donna Caponi certainly wasn't any Slow-Play Fay or Play-Slow Flo. She was hard at work on a 71. Glen Campbell, the celeb, was in the process of carving out a surprising 72. When I finally started helping, our team chewed its way down to serious under-par figures. My moment of real glory came at the 13th when I got into a good drive, and a decent eight-iron, and then casually dropped a 15-footer for a birdie. Smoking. Donna raced over and gave me a birdie kiss, the crowd clapped, Glen patted me on the damp sweater and I looked around for the wife. Wasn't there, naturally. Had gone to get another Coke. Figured.

You blew my birdie back there, I told her.

"Well, thank goodness for *something* good," she said. "I just wish you hadn't picked *today* to play so badly."

Hold it, I said. It's not all that bad. I'll be about an 82 with a triple bogey and a double bogey. Take away those two holes and . . .

"Glen's played just great all the way," she said.

. . . it's down to about a 77 or so, which isn't all that . . .

"He's really hit some wonderful shots."

. . . bad, actually. And I've made a few pars. It isn't exactly like I never hit a single . . .

"I love his shirt and pants. Aren't they good-looking?"

. . . shot, all day long. I mean, it's not exactly my *profession*, playing golf. Considering that I only play . . .

"Did he say he'd get us a table for his opening tonight at the International?"

. . . a few times a year, living in Fun City, whereas certain show-biz guys don't have anything to do but play a guitar and hang around Riviera and Lakeside . . .

"Isn't he the cutest thing? And so nice and friendly."

. . . and, anyhow, you sure missed seeing a good birdie back there.

Nobody I've ever known in my entire life has ever won a Pro-Am. I have played in maybe 7,895 of them over the past 25 years, with any number of fine partners – guys who could really play and guys who had a bundle of strokes to use – and I have very often been "the leader in the clubhouse," as the TV commentators say, but before nightfall every one of these Pro-Ams has been won by a bunch of guys from Sacramento or Tampa. The pro would be an unknown, and his amateur partners would consist of a real-estate developer, an electrical contractor and a priest. They would be 24 under par.

Obviously, then, it was quite silly for Donna Caponi, Glen Campbell or me to think that our measly little round of 14-under would win anything on that first day. And of course it didn't. Marilynn Smith had a team that featured Jerry Lucas, the basketball star, who went out with his 12 handicap and shot a two-under 70 – gross – just like most of the 12-handicappers I ever knew back in Texas. They won laughing.

At the daily cocktail party and prize-giving, where all the Sealy folks got to work on their autograph collections and wondered where Joe Namath was, Jerry Lucas apologised and Donna Caponi confided that she was taking a party of 12 to both Glen Campbell shows that night.

For Friday's round the dummy got himself a golf shirt, his wife stayed at poolside, he drew for a pro a nice young married lady from Midland, Texas named Judy Rankin who had captured three L.P.G.A. tournaments last year, and, for his other partner, a guy from Tampa with a long drive and a lot of strokes. Guy named Bill. Land developer. I thought we were a lock.

For a long time we were. Bill from Tampa was a cheer-leader who called our pro "Judy, baby", and liked to take out a nine-iron for a five-iron shot and announce, "If it's only 170 yards, a nine's plenty for me, baby."

We played the back nine first and didn't cause any particular commotion until the 18th (our ninth) when I did one of those

things we all did every week when we were 15 years old. I holed out a chip shot for an eagle.

From up on the TV tower, where the Hughes Network people were rehearsing, Bob Toski was giggling. "Where'd you learn that?" he called down. "In a subway?"

Our gallery consisted primarily of one: Walter (Yippy) Rankin, Judy's husband, a golf widower, a big, good-natured guy.

Somewhere on the incoming nine, Yippy Rankin made the mistake of telling us, "You know, you-all are 15-under and that's leading. I think you can win it today."

The ninth hole at The Desert Inn course (which would be our last) is an unprintable annoyance as far as I'm concerned. You have two choices off the tee on this par-four. You can drive it into a pond on the left or out of bounds into some homes on the right.

Knowing we had it all wrapped up, then, Judy Rankin promptly hit her drive into the pond, and I promptly hit mine out of bounds. None of this seemed to bother Bill from Tampa, however. He just stepped up and split the fairway with a boomer. Nine-iron to the green.

"I'll handle it, baby," he said.

When we reached Bill from Tampa's tee shot, we could see the scoreboard and absorb the fact that our team *was* leading. I reminded our partner that he had a stroke on the hole, on top of everything else, so there was no point in being brave. Just a little flip up there to the big, safe part of the green and two putts would give us 16-under, more than we needed. That'll be a sweet $500 for Judy Rankin and some Steuben for the good guys.

"Don't worry, I'll put her right up there, baby," said Bill from Tampa.

Who cold-bladed it out of bounds, and we finished tied for second.

90

Saturday's round was fairly uneventful, except for the fact that I was paired with some of the best set decoration on the new ladies' tour. She was Donna's sister, Janet Caponi, who wears hot pants and helps make the L.P.G.A. look a lot different from the way I remembered it. Donna had taken the lead in the Sealy Classic itself, and we spent a lot of time asking for reports on her round. It was hot and windy, and the round passed as slowly as you might guess it would for somebody who had now been in Las Vegas for five days, which is the equivalent of 17 years. I was sadly over-Bill Cosby-d, over-Juliet Prowse-d, over-dinner-and-late-show-d, over-black jack-d and soundly asleep on each and every backswing.

John Montgomery and Bud Erickson decided that I created something of a minor problem for Sunday's final round. They had quite an athletic event on their hands, what with Donna Caponi holding a one-stroke lead over Janie Blalock, who had a sweet personality and a fine, fine game, and Sandra Palmer, an old friend of mine, as it happened, from Texas, who had yet to win her first tournament. And bunched together right behind them were all of the other top lady pros: Sandra Haynie, who had just won three in a row, Marlene Hagge, Jo Ann Prentice, Kathy Whitworth, Peggy Wilson, Pam Barnett, Margie Masters, Judy Rankin and Carol Mann.

Not only were the girls going out there on Sunday and battling it out for what was a big pay day for them, they were going to have to play threesomes: two lady pros with one celeb of sorts. For example, Montgomery and Erickson (and Sealy) thought it would be nifty for national television if there was a Glen Campbell or Joe Namath in every group of girls. And no writers.

"Let's face it," Bud Erickson told me. "You're not much of a TV attraction."

Just blurt it out, Bud I said. No need to doll it up.

"How about 7.37 a.m. with Mary Lou Daniel and Jan Ferraris?"

I said I thought I'd be off the tables by then. Fine.

Part of the Sunday offering to keep the men stimulated, was a competition for a huge chunk of Steuben shaped into the form of a trophy. The Heart of Variety Cup, they called it. A man took his handicap and used it, and took the best holes he could get from his

91

two lady pros, and all of that counted as *his* score, best ball.

Inasmuch as I was a dew sweeper that Sunday, Mary Lou and Jan and I got around rather swiftly. In fact, we finished at 11 o'clock just as Donna Caponi, Janie Blalock and Glen Campbell were teeing off. Mary Lou and Jan had been excellent companions and pretty impressive shotmakers. I must admit.

Maybe I particularly liked the two of them because I beat them with a light-running 75 from memory. In any case, our combined scores gave me eight-under for the round, and I was the leader in the clubhouse.

When you finish early you get to be the leader in the clubhouse for quite a long time. At The Desert Inn, I suppose I was the leader in the clubhouse for, oh, three or four hours. As a matter of fact, I was the leader in the clubhouse for so long that I finally started worrying that I might win.

There is no rule, of course, which says the leader in the clubhouse can't leave the clubhouse. So I went out on the course to watch Donna, Janie and Sandra Palmer throw the lead in the Sealy back and forth in pure melodramatic fashion. Hell of a tournament. They were each making one immense pressure shot after another while the Namaths and Campbells tried to stay out of the way.

Presently, after glancing at a scoreboard, I realised that I was a *co*-leader in the clubhouse.

Then it all fell apart. Namath, Mantle and Campbell went by me, and then here came Don Adams with 18 strokes and a couple of pretty fair partners in Sandra Haynie and Marlene Hagge. He would win by a stroke.

"You're tied for fifth in the clubhouse," my wife said.

The Sealy-L.P.G.A. Classic came down to the very last hole where Sandra Palmer, who had never won a tournament, held a one-stroke lead over Donna Caponi, directly behind her. As Sandra hit her second shot into a front bunker by the 18th green, Donna smashed a big drive down the fairway. Everybody figured it would go into sudden death.

I curiously found myself standing out there half-way up the fairway watching both, pulling for both; for my old friend Sandra from the old home town, the ex-college cheerleader whom I had first seen play when she was 14; and for my new friend, Donna, the dancer, in many ways the solidest player of all the girls.

My wife said, "You've got to admit this is pretty exciting."

Big deal, I said. Ten thousand dollars. Nicklaus gets that much for marking his ball.

"You're phony," she said.

Yeah, I know, I said. But keep it in the family. It's an image deal.

About then, Sandra Palmer hit a slightly stupendous bunker shot that took two hops and rolled straight into the cup for an eagle 3; for all of the whoops, all of the glory and the biggest chunk of the cash. For victory.

I saw her later. She was still in semi-shock from her first win.

"Did you have fun?" Sandra asked. "I hope you got to see that we have lots and lots of really fine players out here and some awfully nice people."

That's true, I said.

"It's great you could be here. I hope a lot of the girls have told you that," Sandra said.

They had, and it was embarrassing.

"See you again somewhere?"

I grinned and said I'd have to check the towns first. See what the bus schedules were like.

Sandra laughed.

"We'll see you again," she said.

Reprinted by permission from *Sports Illustrated*, August 9, 1971. © Time Inc. 1971.

II
Anatomy of a Big Hit

by Keith Mackie

In the days before the world became accustomed to the awesome power of the Jack Nicklaus brand of golf, a giant Welshman was booming 300-yard drives down the fairways of Britain. The operative words being "down the fairways", for Dave Thomas had mastered the art of hitting the ball a long, long way with deadly accuracy.

Although now semi-retired from tournament golf, a situation accelerated by a back injury and Thomas's highly successful golf-course design business in company with Peter Alliss, he can still hit the ball as well as ever –

and still with the same unerring pin-point precision.

The picture sequence study on the following pages clearly shows the Thomas formula for long, straight hitting. There is something to be learned here by every class of golfer.

From an early stage of his golfing career Thomas found it easy to hit the ball hard and still keep it in play. Yet during the Centenary Open at St. Andrews in 1964 Norman Von Nida suggested a very slight change in Thomas's grip. This had repercussions throughout his swing and made an im-

mediate difference of between 10 and 15 yards off the tee.

At that time Thomas was showing only one and a half knuckles on the left hand, and at address his hands were held very high. Von Nida suggested that he should drop his hands a little and get his left hand slightly more on top of the shaft to show two and a half knuckles. The out-of-bounds is all down the right-hand side at St. Andrews and this new set-up gave him a bigger turn away from the ball and made the swing a little flatter, causing a slight draw.

Gradually he settled down with this new method and that was what caused the change from being naturally long and straight to hitting the ball very long. It made a difference of 10–15 yards right away on normal drives.

The seemingly insignificant change in his grip made a difference throughout Thomas's swing. He had always stood very close to the ball and swung very upright, but by dropping his hands at address and moving his left hand more on top of the shaft he moved slightly further away from the ball and swung flatter and with a bigger turn.

As far as Thomas is concerned, confidence in the ability to contact the ball squarely and solidly is the greatest factor in big hitting. A long drive is chiefly a question of generating sufficient clubhead speed at impact, and the more confidence you have in your swing the more you are able really to let fly at the ball.

Unfortunately, there is no easy, over-night way to hit 300-yard tee shots. Thomas warns that confidence in the swing can only be built through practice and the achievement of a basically sound method. He doesn't believe that the average club golfer can expect to hit the ball flat out because he does not play sufficient golf to have the required confidence in his swing.

Thomas stands to the ball with his right foot drawn back slightly, closing the stance a little, but still with the right foot pointing directly forward, not turned outwards. By pulling the right foot back he gets an easier and more comfortable turn away from the ball.

Aiming the shot is very important. Ten chances to one if it is lined up over the left shoulder at address the ball will be hit right of the target. The correct way is to approach the ball from behind, place the clubhead in position and then take up the stance, with the right foot pointing in a line parallel to the club shaft and left arm. The shoulders and hips then cross these lines at right angles.

At the start of the swing the club should never be taken away from the ball fast, but should be under complete control, with the hands, arms and club moving back in one piece. But this should not be exaggerated and the wrists should start to cock before the clubhead has been taken back too far. Above all, the club should not be snatched away from the address position, for this will cut

down the shoulder turn and move the whole body out of position.

Resist any temptation to overswing in an effort to get more length, but get the shoulders fully turned without turning the hips too far. A big hip turn will only give trouble because it necessitates a large movement at the start of the downswing to get back into a good impact position. Restrict the hip turn, but really wind up the shoulders, getting round so that the left shoulder points down at the ball.

All through the backswing you should have the feeling of "sitting" on the right leg and turn round that set-up. Such a feeling gives a firm foundation from which to unleash the hands and arms into the ball.

Don't get the left heel too far off the ground in the backswing as this will tend to cause a sway. By bending the right knee the left heel can be kept down, making a very firm basis for the swing.

Have the impression of swinging into the ball from behind, along the line of flight. Never feel that you are hitting down on the ball.

Thomas recommends Arnold Palmer's advice about hitting the ball hard right from the start and then learning to hit it straight. Two or three lessons are essential at the beginning to ensure a good grip and correct set-up, but once these have been mastered, just hit the ball hard. It's the only way to make it go a long way.

12

Long Live Match-play!

by Mike Stevenson

That most genuine and genial of characters, Bill Ferguson, professional at Ilkley Golf Club, warmed the cockles of this particular heart just after he'd been knocked out of another match-play championship!

"We must try hard not to forget that golf is still only a game," he said, and if the words do not strike you at once as of earth-shattering significance, pause a moment and ponder them. Modern golf appears to me to have become a monstrous juggernaut of sponsorship (however vital), endorsements, television appeal, incredibly huge rewards for a successful player and, above all, predictably related stress and tension, leading in extreme cases to actual illness.

I talked to one young ex-pro recently who had been a fine amateur golfer. He won £280 as against £1,500 expenses in under two years on the circuit and acquired an ulcer in the process all by the advanced age of 22. The race will not always go to the swift in golf but rather to the tough.

No wonder most of the pros don't like match-play. I talked to Bernard Gallacher about this very subject recently and he spoke, I imagine, for the majority of his colleagues. "Match-play just isn't fair. I may go round in 65 but if someone burns it up in 64 against me, I'm out." With Merit and Ryder Cup points at stake in addition to the vast sums of prize-money involved this is both a predictable and entirely forgivable attitude.

Yet I think it is a mistaken one. Speaking as one who was bored almost to tears by the so-called "computerised test match" some time ago, I want to see more of the element of personal confrontation and individual character in sport – not less. It is the grim-faced anonymity and inarticulacy of some of their colleagues that has made the verbal gymnastics of M. Ali and L. Trevino not to mention F. Trueman so widely enjoyed and universally news-worthy.

Ultimately it is the paying customer who will decide and the massive popularity of the Piccadilly World Match-play Championship clearly speaks for itself in this context. It is common knowledge that Trevino's tor-

"OLD" WILLIE DUNN, *who featured with his brother in a big-money match against* ALLAN ROBERTSON *and* TOM MORRIS *over three courses in 1849. In the days when a labourer earned 10 shillings a week, this match was played for stakes of £400.*

"YOUNG" WILLIE DUNN, *"Old" Willie's son and first winner of the American Open Championship at Shinnecock Hills in 1894.*

rent of quips and quiddities, interspersed with fierce concentration when *he* played his shots, threw Tony Jacklin's own confidence and concentration on at least one occasion, largely one presumes because he allowed himself to get irritated; but has there ever been finer golf than that produced by these two players in the semi-final of the Match-play in 1972. Two superb soloists each able to display that much more virtuosity owing to the other's influence?

There's another point. Some of the most dramatic moments of medal play result directly from the sort of problem which is the

bone and sinew of match-play. As early as 1896 the legendary Harry Vardon knew all about such things. Playing the 18th at Muir-field, he knew that he needed a four to beat J. H. Taylor's aggregate of 316. A five would earn him the right of a play-off and the green was guarded by a deep bunker. If he finished in the bunker a six would probably result but if he carried it – his first Open Championship. It was not entirely characteristic that Vardon chose to play safe for his five and beat "J.H." in the 36-hole play-off, at the end of which, with Vardon three strokes ahead at the 18th, "J.H." was confronted

DICKIE DUNN, *"Young" Willie's son and surviving member of a great golfing family.*

with the same problem that had faced his opponent in the championship proper. This time, of course, Taylor had to go for the carry, failed, and Harry Vardon had won the Open.

But I haven't come to my main point yet. Tradition must not be regarded as sacrosanct for that way lies ossification, but by the same token change is equally dangerous for its own sake. I believe that the old Scots tradition of match-play golf, allied to fanatical partisanship and, in the days when a pint of beer was a halfpenny, huge sums at stake, must have produced some of the most fascinating contests in the history of the game.

One such match was played 124 years ago on the testing and attractive North Berwick course which then consisted of seven holes to be played five times plus one additional hole for a 36-hole contest. This means, of course, that the drama in question occurred on the area now comprising the 18th around the present clubhouse. But let John Kerr, compiler and editor of *The Golf-Book of East Lothian*, printed in 1896 and my principal source for information concerning this remarkable match, set the scene.

"At an early stage in the history of the North Berwick club we are also introduced to a quartette of heroes, of whose renown all golf-books speak at length, Allan Robertson, whom some call the greatest golfer that ever lived; his pupil, Tom Morris, still alive, and known to all as the G.O.M. of professionals; and the brothers Willie and Jamie Dunn. Perhaps the most notable match in the history of golf was that between Allan and Old Tom against the Dunn brothers in 1849, which was played over Musselburgh, the home green of the Dunns, St. Andrew's, the home green of their opponents, and North Berwick as neutral ground. At Musselburgh, the Dunns were victorious by 13 up and 12

99

to play; at St. Andrews, Tom and Allan won by a narrow majority. Like the election of Lord Rector by 'nations' at the Universities of Glasgow and Edinburgh, this match was decided by greens and not by the aggregate of holes, so North Berwick was the scene of the decisive match."

I am now indebted to a Mr. Peters who writes of this match in a book entitled *Reminiscences of Golf and Golfers* from which Mr. Kerr quotes. It appears that all the world and his wife turned up at North Berwick for the big match and each side had his following of dedicated fanatics. "The twa Dunnies", as the brothers were known, were supported by the clubmaster to the Honourable Company of Edinburgh Golfers, John Gourlay, one who, as a maker of the leather and feather ball used before the advent of the gutty, was regarded as unparalleled.

In a strong wind blowing from the southwest, the Dunn brothers appeared to be racing away with the match. Mr. Peters reports that: "The Dunns' driving, in fact, completely overpowered their opponents. They went sweeping over hazards which the St. Andrews man had to play short of." At lunch, the Dunns were (like Trevino on a different occasion!) four up and long odds were being offered on them.

After lunch the game swung further in favour of the Dunns but Tom Morris was in no way despairing. Someone said to him: "Tom, you're going to get beaten." He replied with words that might well be advantageously engraved on every golfer's heart: "I'm not so sure of that. The Dunnies are playing a game nae man can beat, an' they may fa' off, but there's nae fear o' Allan an' me fa'in off."

Like skilled swordsmen who wait the slightest sign of frailty in respected opponents, Tom Morris and Allan Robertson kept on playing their own game until oppotunity befriended them, and befriend them it did. The tide began to turn when a certain Captain Campbell of Schiehallion was heard to utter the epic pronouncement: "Gad, sir. If they take another hole they'll win the match." Morris and Robertson duly obliged so that, with two holes to play, the game was all square.

It was at this juncture that the game firmly entered the realms of the improbable. After their drives, Robertson's ball was in a poor lie and the Dunns considerably further and lying well. After Allan and Tom had played three more they were bunkered close to the green, while the Dunns' ball had come to rest on an unmetalled cart-track, snug up against a sea boulder which some impish Caledonian poltergeist had placed there for their undoing. The Dunns consulted Sir David Baird, the umpire, and were informed that the offending stone could not be removed with a spade as they had suggested, a decision that caused the peppery Jamie Dunn to become gripped with fury. His illustration of the old saying: "Lose your temper and lose the match" could not have been bettered.

One of the Dunns, history does not tell us which, struck at the ball with his iron and hit the top of the stone. The other did the same and his partner made another desperate effort to dislodge the ball before the simple expedient, that, adopted initially would have won them the match, was performed: the ball was struck with the back of an iron onto grass beyond the track but the damage had been done and both the hole and the match lost.

The stake played for in this incredible match was £400 and when one recalls that a labourer or farm worker was earning around 10 shillings per week then, quite apart from the huge sums wagered by supporters, the magnitude of the occasion will be clear.

And how vividly the character and personality of the "Twa Dunnies" speak to us down the intervening years and how vibrantly alive are the features that we see in the primitive photos reproduced in the *Golf-Book of East Lothian*. Old Willie Dunn with firm jaw and kindly twinkling eyes contrasts with the similar yet dissimilar countenance of his brother, whose mouth and eyes are etched with more passionate and less relaxed lines.

Old Willie became as much a legend in his own time as a club-maker, as he had been as a player and not the least of his distinctions was that his son "Young" Willie Dunn in 1894 became the first American Open Champion. He counted among his friends John D. Rockefeller, John L. Sullivan and "Buffalo" Bill, not to mention Zane Gray with whom he used to go tarpon fishing in Florida!

"Young" Willie's son was himself a golfer of distinction who continued the family tradition of colourful and zestful living. Dickie Dunn, now in his 82nd year, lives at Barmby Moor in East Yorkshire and a more warm-hearted and vital person I have yet to meet. Dickie is far from well now but his eyes light up with his grandfather's twinkle at recollection of the soubriquet bestowed upon him by his friend J. S. F. Morrison, who called him "Yorks and Corks" when he was Yorkshire champion and changed it to "Lincs and Drinks" when he became Lincolnshire champion!

Dickie was a beautiful striker of the ball who should have played for England far more than he did, his only appearance being against Ireland at Dollymount, where he had the misfortune (or lack of foresight) to turn up wearing his Leinster Regiment tie. The hospitality that he received meant that he was in no fit state to do himself justice and, not surprisingly, was not asked to represent his country again. One can almost hear "Young" Willie's chuckles!

Coming as he does from one of the world's oldest and most distinguished golfing families, Dickie Dunn's golf has been match-play, with the game mattering more than the result, however keenly that game may have been contested. We don't visualise Old Willie and the irascible Jamie Dunn bemoaning the fact that defeat at the hands of Morris and Robertson had robbed them of the chance of earning an honest bob or two endorsing haggis or sporrans. We see them, surely, after the smoke had settled and Jamie had calmed down a little, looking at each other sadly, shaking their heads and saying plaintively: "Man, were we no the daftest ever?"

We are descended, so we are told, from hunters. If modern sport is a war substitute as one must be forgiven for supposing when watching some of the uninhibited football matches of recent times, then let match-play golf be a hunt substitute with hunter and quarry acting and reacting one upon the other.

One of the greatest medal players in the world understands all about this. Lee Trevino said in the context of his astonishing defeat of Tony Jacklin in the 1972 Piccadilly World Match-play: "When a man knows he's playing somebody who's playing good, it gets him going a little bit better." Hardly deathless prose but he's got a point.

Less match-play? Rubbish! Let's have more – and let's be sure that, before we scrap traditions that have stood the test of the years, we have something preferable to put in their place.

Jack Nicklaus

"Just because I like to fish and escape at regular intervals it does not mean that I no longer enjoy the game. I think I enjoy it more these days and feel the Grand Slam in one year is possible and that I can do it."

"I don't think I can ever be another Arnold Palmer. No one could. He can hitch up his pants or yank on a glove and people will start oohing and aahing. When I hitch up mine, nobody notices. I envy him, sure, but there's no way I can be like him in this respect. I just have to be myself."

"My main objective in golf is to win as many major titles as I can around the world. That is what keeps me going and what I imagine will always be my strongest incentive."

"I play best from the square position, not bad from the open position and almost always poorly when I fall into a closed position. I think most other golfers have the same experience."

"I can control my life pretty well. I like to do business because I like to use my mind other than on a golf course. But there's room for both if you organise yourself properly."

"I see putting as a matter of feel and I'm not sure you can get that through practice. Just working away on a practice green doesn't help me much. To benefit from practice I have to concentrate and I find this difficult with putting."

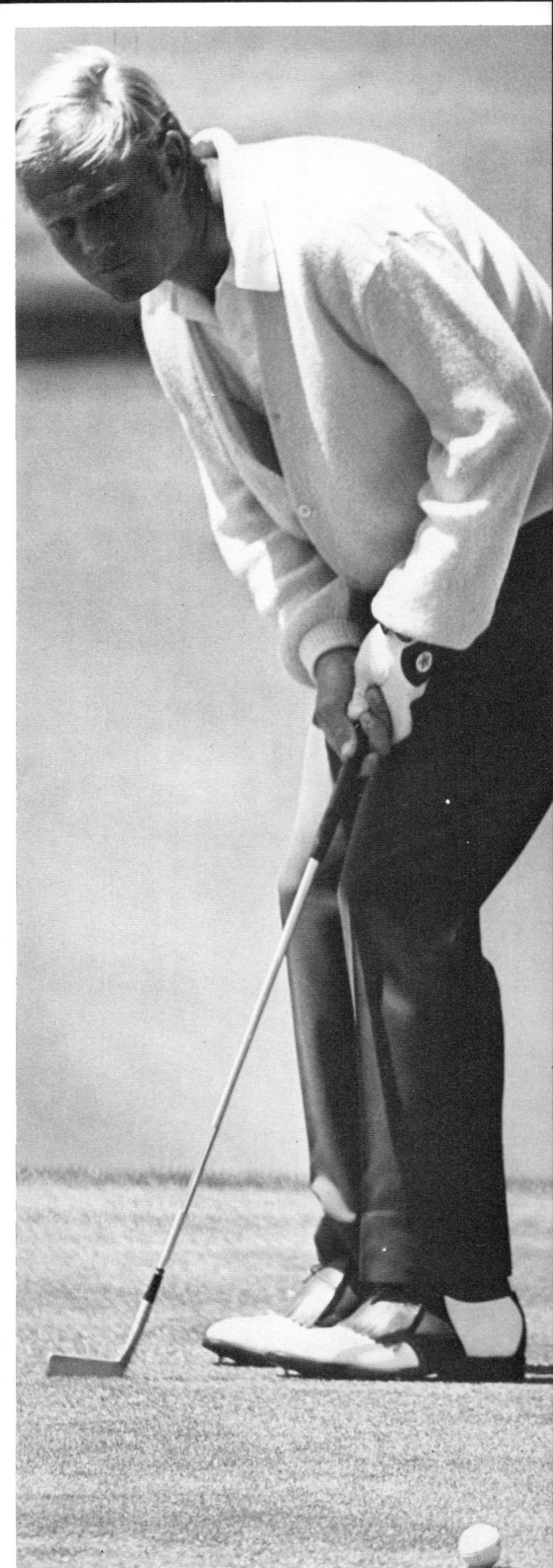

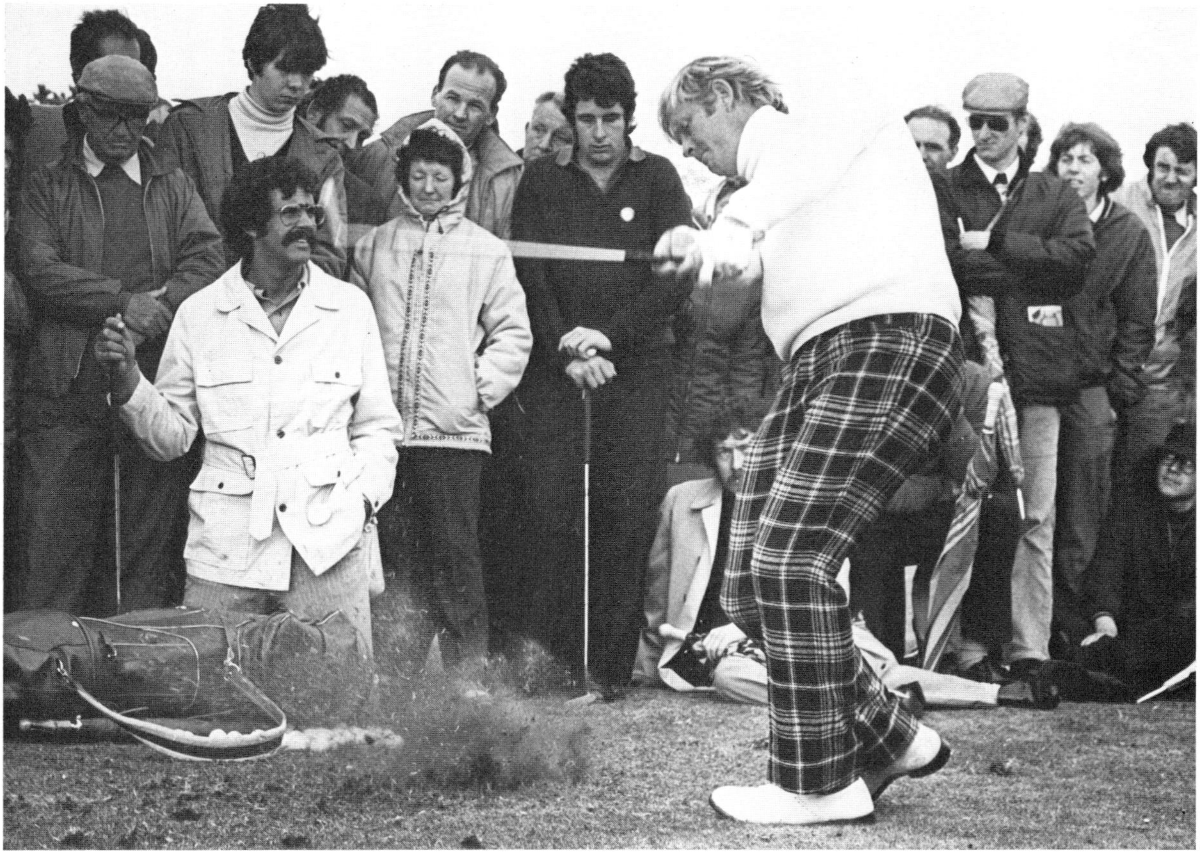

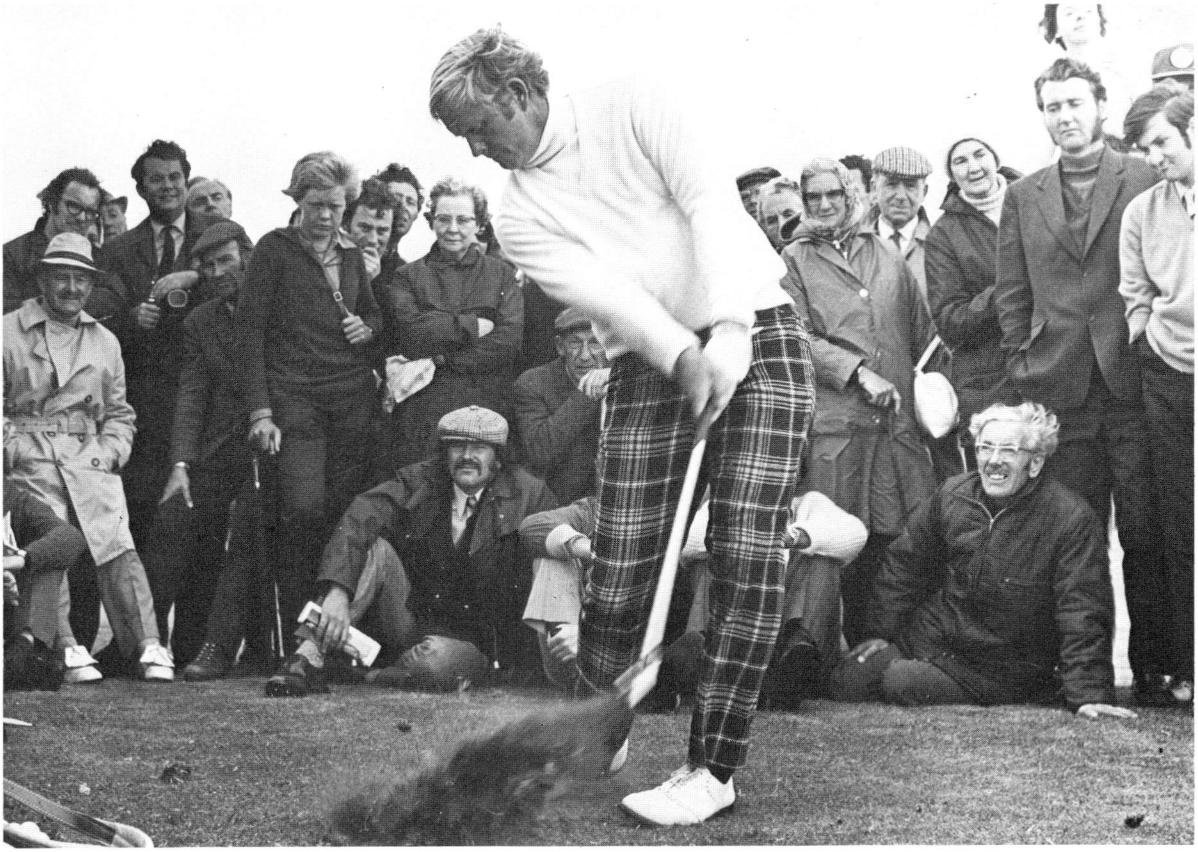

14 Shots I have Hit and

by Ray Jacobs

"Change," said a French monarch, who knew a thing or two about such matters, "is the greatest aphrodisiac of all." It has always seemed to me that the most stimulating effect of golf on those who court its fickle nature is the apparently inexhaustible variety of its attractions.

The most obvious of these are the total contrasts offered by the actual settings for the game. There are simply no two courses of a kind, even though their nature may be similar – links, park or heath. The atmosphere and the immediate surroundings are certainly different at Wembley, Hampden, and San Siro; but only the dimensions of a football pitch vary, for the same lines are drawn wherever the game is played.

Has there ever been a game like golf for the amount of time and money devoted to the development of the equipment used for playing it? Footballers may now be wearing boots that are like carpet slippers compared with the steel-toed monstrosities of scarcely a generation ago, but for devotion to the task of making last year's model of club or ball obsolete, or seem that way, this year golf's manufacturers need to take lessons only from their car-making brothers.

From that aspect of the game it is only a short step to the willingness of golfers themselves to be mesmerised by the claims of this equipment maker that his clubs offer a more extensive "sweet spot" and that, therefore, there is a better chance of catching one on the meat, or another who asserts that his ball will fly further. Nothing will do but that we seekers after the elusive truth rush to put the words to the test.

Next, after we have kitted ourselves out with these supposed cures for all ills, there is no lack of advice telling us – metaphorically, of course – what to do with it all. With the possible exception of the quantity of counsel

106

Missed

An eight-hour time difference and a nagging deadline made golf writer RAYMOND JACOBS *miss the historic shot with which* JACK NICKLAUS *almost holed in one at the 17th hole at Pebble Beach, California, in the final round of the 1972 U.S. Open.*

available to those with a trouble love-life no group of people have submitted themselves to instruction as eagerly and hopefully – not to mention trustfully – as golfers.

It is little wonder, all things considered, that bars the length and breadth of the country resound with tales of horror, mystery and suspense. To be sure, there are only a few activities more tedious than listening to somebody else's golf story, especially when your own is obviously twice as worth the telling. Running it close are such themes as – "How I knocked five minutes off my previous best time motoring from Glasgow to London" – or "What I told the managing director the company should do to increase productivity."

Therefore, with an inexorable logic which by now you may have seen coming like a telegraphed punch, I propose to relate some of the more bizarre experiences that have happened to me on the golf course during a career whose modest achievements have earned exactly the reward they have deserved – complete anonymity. The only excuse for this infliction is that even my humble contributions in this direction do at least support what I was saying at the start about golf's infinite variety.

These arresting accounts will not only deal with shots I have hit myself, but shots others have hit. Some of the latter I missed, a riddle easily explained by the fact that I was not there at the time, having been guided by an infallible instinct to another part of the course. Others I did see, in whole or in part, either by happy accident or because the situation left me no alternative but to be where it was all at, or being got together – or one of those other indispensable phrases I don't know how we ever did without.

I concede this to be a risky project. Indeed, your mind may have already tuned out, your eyes glazed over, and your fingers be moving the page in search of another chapter. But with luck, like P. G. Wodehouse's immortal character, The Oldest Member, I have caught you by the sleeve of your jacket. You are held in your chair, admitting with an ill-concealed foreboding that you have, indeed, heard none of these stories, to which I reply, in the way of The Oldest Member, "Be of good cheer, you are about to hear them now!"

There have been countless thousands of holes-in-one, but to make such a stroke successfully is such an outrageous fluke, probably the greatest in all sport, that I imagine they have all had one factor in common – their unexpectedness. They must catch everyone completely unawares. The deed is over and done with so quickly, and anyway the odds against are so great, that bemusement and disbelief rather than elation are the immediate reactions.

I have been at the firing end of one – at the eighth hole on the championship course at Carnoustie, which seems to me to be a place a cut above the ordinary for perpetrating the feat – and the other people who happened to be around at the time got themselves into a more excited condition on my behalf than I could muster myself. Possibly the thought of the subsequent cost of the obligatory celebrations was an immediately sobering influence.

To be at the receiving end of a hole-in-one is just as startling, perhaps even more so. During the 1972 Youths' Championship at Glasgow Gailes a ball pitched beyond the 15th hole by a yard and abruptly screwed back in. As someone said at the time: "There it was, gone!" But at least one had seen the unlikely trick turned. On two other occasions, both historic in their way, I heard rather than saw the incident, although for both I was close to the scene.

Standing half-way down the 16th hole at Royal St. George's when Tony Jacklin holed out on his way to winning the Dunlop Masters was exactly the wrong place to be. As it turned out, one was so near and yet further away than one knew. The ball disappeared all right, but for me behind an intervening bank, and so what millions miles away saw clearly on their television screens others, like myself within a few yards of the scene, witnessed only later on the recordings.

As if that were not irritating enough, another writer and myself only narrowly missed being present when John Hudson hit the bull's eye with consecutive barrels during the second round of the 1971 Martini Tournament, the first time this had been done in a major professional event. From a distance we casually observed the reaction to Hudson's holing out at the 11th. "Good for him," we remarked and went on our way, for Hudson was not among the leaders. Whereupon his driver obliged at the very next hole and Hudson's name and achievement were indelibly in the record books.

It's certainly an irritation when sheer miscalculation or the exigencies of daily journalism stop one being more often an eyewitness to an exciting run of scoring, or a shot that decides a major championship. On such occasions there is nothing to do but to bite the bullet and hope that at another time, in another place, the scales will balance out and there will be something else to store in memory's deposit account.

An eight-hour time difference and a nagging deadline made me an unwilling absentee from the short 17th at Pebble Beach, when in the final round of the 1972 U.S. Open Championship Jack Nicklaus made sure of equalling Bobby Jones's record of 13 major titles by almost holing out a one-iron shot into the wind at this difficult and treacherous hole. And it was about a year after the Open Championship at Muirfield that I at last saw on film Lee Trevino outrageously chip in at the 71st, thus making Jacklin lose the lead he seemed certain to take into the final hole, to which I had hurried in the confident hope of seeing his second triumph in three years duly acclaimed.

St. Andrews was the scene of one more instance of a lost opportunity, but of another happily found. The only hole I saw of Jacklin's astounding 29 to the turn in the 1970 Open, was the first. Here he gained what was to be the first of five birdies. I finally saw the eagle two with which he completed the outward half, months later on the film of the Championship. For me sudden-death play-offs and matches that go to extra holes are invariably mundane and an anti-climax to the preceding battle. But since Charlie Green was defending the Scottish amateur title and was having to go beyond the 18th, duty called – and Green rewarded me by playing a match-winning shot at the 20th, picking the ball off a gravel path with an eight-iron and hitting it to within four feet of the hole from a distance of about 140 yards.

Playing from strange places is the perennial lot of the handicap golfer, whose unpredictable sense of direction it is impossible for any

When NICKLAUS *hit his classic shot on the way to victory in the 1972 U.S. Open as described in this chapter, he was also on the way to equalling* BOBBY JONES's *record of victory in 13 major championships. Jones, shown here, quit big-time golf in 1930 after winning the British and American Amateur and Open Championships in one season.*

109

Shots I have Hit and Missed

course architect to take completely into account. Foursomes golf, truly a game within a game, tends to produce situations which are not only weird but really eccentric. This habit was brought home forcefully once, when my partner found himself playing our side's third shot at the first at Old Prestwick at a point further away from the hole than we had started. Of course, it was all his fault. He had nobbled his drive into such a bad lie in heather that the only way for me to redeem it was to play out backwards.

Then there was the time I hooked a drive off the seventh tee at the Glasgow Club's Killermont course over a fence towards a row of houses. It was one of those moments when you do not look after the flight of the ball, you listen. The distinctive sound of breaking glass informed me of the landing area the ball had found. Fortunately the club was insured against the worst excesses of its members.

But without question the finest single achievement of an erratic golfing career was to make six at the last hole at St. Andrews after the ball had, temporarily, been twice out of play. The scenario was as follows: Topped drive into Swilcan Burn. Pick out and hit third beyond road. Take about two clubs too many and hit approach that was still rising as it passed over the green. Ball hits stone monument and rebounds over heads of scattering, startled, spectators back onto green. Two putts.

Finally, there was a singular, though brief, moment of glory. For the first, and so far only, time I played in a Pro-Am. During three holes, over which I received three shots, I improved on my professional partner's score by no fewer than five strokes. He was not noticeably pleased. Smiling through cold teeth, he said: "Let me know when you need any help." Needless to say, that was the

110

LEE TREVINO *chips into the 71st hole, the shot which allowed him to retain his Open Championship title against Tony Jacklin and Jack Nicklaus at Muirfield in 1972.*

end of my contribution, but we won a prize and I felt my efforts had been flatteringly recognised when the lady presenting it tried to give me the cheque instead of the half-dozen tumblers that kept my amateur status uncorrupted. Sprightly footwork and a long reach got the professional to the slim white envelope first only by a short finger-nail.

Years ago someone wrote defending golf from the accusation that it was a dangerous sport. "I have been hit," he protested, "only two or three times during the last year." Goodness knows, there are plenty of examples listed in *The Golfer's Handbook*, but it has always amazed me that there have not been more accidents, fatal and otherwise, on golf courses. Having endangered the life and limb of other innocent bystanders over a misspent golfing life, I suppose it was only natural justice that I should have my own put in extreme danger.

None other than Peter Oosterhuis was the culprit. At the last hole at Fulford he hooked from the tee and while others went rapidly to ground at the shouts of "Fore!" I stood mine and was rewarded for my un-flinching trust that it couldn't happen to me by being struck a smart crack across the leg. I know that Peter from time to time lets one get away in the grand manner, but 40 yards off his intended line seemed a safe distance to be standing. Still, you never can tell.

At least Oosterhuis did not, like Freddie Tait towards the end of the last century, drive a ball through a man's hat – a tall one, I presume. The damage apparently cost Tait all of five shillings, a sum he thought excessive. The incident, however, was put thoroughly in perspective by Old Tom Morris, who growled unsympathetically: "Eh, Mr. Tait, you ought to be glad it was only a new hat you had to buy, and not an oak coffin!" Amen to that.

15

My Best and Worst Holes

by Iain Crawford

The last time I counted I had played more than 450 golf courses – a monumental waste of time, you may say, but by no means a record. One American golf nut has topped 3,000. Although down the years I have written about a lot of the courses I have played around the world, all of them were played for fun. The way I play golf it has to be fun, otherwise I would have committed hara-kiri decades ago.

Most of the courses I have played gave me a lot pleasure and if you know many of them and agree with my rather arbitrary choice of the nine worst holes and the nine best holes I shall be astounded.

For golf is essentially a game of mood and weather as well as skill and the lie of the land. The hole which is a menace today can be a joy tomorrow. So any choice of this kind has to be very personal and highly subjective. Everyone will have their own ideas about where to suffer most and on what greens to preen. These are just mine.

If there has been a criterion of choice it is this. All the 18 best and worst are tough holes. The nine "worst" are those on which I have found it consistently difficult to score well because they seem to me to have features which defeat, frustrate not to say madden the average golfer. The nine best are just as tough but they are the holes on which I have produced that occasional put-together miracle of three to five strokes which keeps us all playing this game. I stand on their tees with a feeling of pleasurable anticipation instead of dread. Every average hacker will know what I mean. The superbly accomplished can stop here. Fellow-tremblers read on.

First the bad ones. They add up to just 3,332 yards, not an excessive length, but their par is 37 which gives some indication of their menace. These may not be the nine worst holes in the world but I would lay fairly substantial odds against anyone coming off the last green with a smug self-satisfied smirk on his face after playing this lot.

Nueva Andalucia, Costa del Sol, Spain. 1st: 401 yards: par-4

This is a golf course designed in the Robert Trent Jones manner which earned him the title of "The Man Who Hates Golfers". It certainly defies the basic rule about courses primarily used by holiday golfers that it has to be fun to play on. There is water, most of it concealed from tee or fairway, at 11 holes. I once played there with an American who lost 15 of his own balls by the 16th and five of mine by the time we reached the last green. Great stuff for aquatic tigers. The first (originally the 10th) is typical. You hit a good drive down the fairway into the middle avoiding the slight crowning which might spill you off into bunkers (three on the left,

112

Troon's eighth hole, an innocent 126 yards from the tee – but danger lurks in deep bunkers on all sides.

Water all the way on the right, with a second shot across a corner of the bay – the third at Great Harbour Cay, Berry Islands, Bahamas.

one on the right). Then you have what looks like a comparatively simple four- or five-iron shot to the raised green, bouncing it just in front and running gently up the slight slope to nestle against the pin if you hit it straight, slightly left of the flag, avoiding the visible bunker on the right. What you don't know until you have hit exactly the shot you planned and had it greeted by a happy cry of "*Agua*" (the theme song of Andalucia), is that there is water all round the green and that the spot on which you planned to bounce your ball is a pond. One of the most molar-grinding starts to a golf course anywhere.

Troon Old Course, Ayrshire, Scotland. 8th: 126 yards: par-3
Statistically a "dawdle" in the Scottish vernacular and the shortest hole in championship golf. But it is not called "the Postage Stamp" for nothing. The green is about the size of a reasonably opulent drawing-room carpet but with rather less nap on it and it gets narrower towards the back. There is a large sand dune to the left, two bunkers below it and another three clustered around the front and left edges. A grassy hump just in front of the green helps to throw you off into the first bunker. With the pin near the front this is a diabolical hole. The first German to play in the Open Championship after the war took 15 here in 1950. The way to play it is to aim for the rear left-hand bunker, not reach it and come back down the slight slope towards the middle of the green.

Pevero, Costa Smeralda, Sardinia. 16th: 316 yards: par-4
This is one of the most beautiful courses I have ever played, greensward carved out of the dramatic mountains behind the luxury rocky coast of the Costa Smeralda, one of the

most spectacular of Europe's playgrounds. The views from almost every hole on this course are breathtaking and Robert Trent Jones's taste for drama is indulged to the full but, for the most part, very fairly. The 16th needs a very carefully placed drive between two lakes which guard the green – one to the left which seems to gather balls off the fairway, and the other in front of the narrow green, over which you have to play your second shot. In addition, the tangle of the macchia scrub and the outcropping rocks crowd in on the fairway, putting accuracy at a premium. Short of the first lake with your drive makes your second shot to the narrow green difficult; even with a longer drive you still have to chip across the lake and hold on the green. Very much a man or mouse hole, this.

La Manga, Costa Blanca, Spain, North Course. 3rd: 500 yards: par-5
La Manga is the new 36-hole golf complex just north of Cartagena on Spain's Costa del Sol. From the sumptuous clubhouse overlooking the valley it looks rather like a thinly planted palm plantation, strangely interspersed with stone-faced ravines and lakes. On the ground it is a much more interesting golfing proposition. The third is a long, tough par-five with a deep ravine cutting across the fairway about the length of a really good drive from the tee. There is a bunker on the right to catch the faded laid-up shot; for your second you have to carry the ravine, a bunch of trees on the right and another lot which thrust onto the fairway from the left, and place your ball with computer-like accuracy between a cluster of five bunkers; then all you have to do is chip onto the green, guarded by a mere three bunkers, and get down in two for your five. Should you achieve this unlikely feat you then have to

play the fourth, a diabolical short hole on a raised green entirely surrounded by ravines and bunkers. Very interesting really, in an infuriating kind of way.

Penina, The Algarve, Portugal. 5th: 509 yards: par-5
Penina was originally a collection of rice fields, therefore when Henry Cotton turned them into a beautifully kept and landscaped golf course, he used a great deal of tortuous ingenuity to make the flat land interesting and to create problems for golfers. The fifth has enough problems to last most courses about half a dozen holes. In the first place there is a stream running diagonally across the fairway, following the right to left line of the dog-leg for the last 300 yards or so all the way up to the green. If you hit a really good one you can be in it by landing in the middle

of the fairway, if you fade your drive you are certain to be in it. With your second shot you have to negotiate an electric pylon in the middle of the fairway while avoiding getting into the stream crossing from right to left. There are bunkers and trees hiding the green tucked right away round the left-hand corner where this particular dog-leg becomes an arthritic claw. Only masterly placement of shots will get you up in three. If you get a five here, walk straight over to the bar between the 11th and 12th and buy yourself a drink. We may never look on your like again.

Bergen Golfklub, Bergen, Norway. 1st: 105 yards: par-3
This is a nine-hole course outside the beautiful port which is the capital of West Norway and as far as I can judge it has been designed

115

to ensure that Norwegians stick to their national sport of skiing. It should not be attempted without crampons and ropes or a short course in mountain warfare. The mile-long walk over a mountain between the sixth and seventh holes is one of the unique features of this course which I look forward eagerly to seeing repeated nowhere. The first is very short and commences from a hearth-rug-sized tee hung precipitously over a lake. Apart from the fact that you feel if you move at all you may well pitch to a watery grave below, you have to carry the lake and a few trees at the other side to reach the green, a simple shot really if you do not have an *acquavit* hangover (inescapable in hospitable Bergen) and are as fearless about heights as a tight-rope walker. Getting down the cliff and across to the green if your ball ever reaches it is another adventure.

Two perfect shots are required to reach this green at the 465-yard 13th on the King's Course at Gleneagles.

Great Harbour Cay, Berry Islands, The Bahamas. 3rd : 365 yards : par-4
This is a quite stunningly lovely course which occupies what seems to be most of the Bahamian island where Jack Nicklaus has a house. Nicklaus comes here mostly to fish, and after playing the third you may well feel tempted to join him. Indeed you can easily be fishing between tee and green, for the sea runs all the way along the right-hand side of the fairway. There are not many problems with bunkers except around the green, but if you do not keep your drive to the left you can very easily find yourself on the beach. With your second shot you have to carry the corner of a bay and stop the ball somehow

116

Killarney's finishing hole – 202 yards surrounded by trees and water.

on a small and fiendishly crowned green. Almost the only friendly gesture is that there are no bunkers in front.

Miami Country Club, West Course, Florida, U.S.A. 13th: 539 yards: par-5
When they used to play the National Airlines Open here this was nearly everyone's unfavourite hole. It is long, there is water all the way on the right, the fairway dog-legs left and narrows just at drive length, with a bunker on the left for added ulcers. The "safe" way into the green is via a crowned fairway which tends to throw the ball into the water which cuts into the hole just in front of the putting surface. There are also

three large bunkers. A birdie on this hole is a *rara avis* for the pros; for my kind of golfer a dodo – extinct.

Royal Birkdale, Southport, Lancashire, England. 6th: 473 yards: par-4
This is one of the greatest English courses, often a site for the Open and full of menacing holes. The sixth is a right-hand dog-leg where you have two blind shots before you get a sight of the green. There is a well-bunkered ridge across the fairway to catch your drive, more ridge on the right making the hole invisible. Unless you carry the fairway ridge with your drive you will not be able to see the green nor the two fearsome bunkers which guard it. But don't worry, you'll find them all right. Not really a par-four for the likes of us whatever the score card says.

117

My Best and Worst Holes

Sweeping aside these admissions of incorrigible rabbithood and a clutch of alienated secretaries and club members, here are nine of the best. These holes have always given me especial pleasure to play, not only because on occasion they have lain within my modest possibilities – some of them in their time have inspired as much terror as any – but I never stand on their tees with anything but a sense of challenge and delight, the prime components of golf.

Sotogrande, Costa del Sol, Spain. 7th: 422 yards: par-4
I have had as much pleasure out of this superb Trent Jones course, the first he designed in Europe, as anywhere I have played. You could choose a dozen holes to praise but the seventh has always seemed to me supreme. It is a left-hand dog-leg, bordered by cork trees and running slightly downhill. Placing your drive is crucial because the second shot has to be played to a very narrow green sloping towards a lake on the right, encircled by bunkers and overhung by trees. You have to hit the green and you have to stay on it. It's a great thrill when you do!

Gleneagles, King's Course, Scotland. 13th: 465 yards: par-4
The two courses at Gleneagles, the King's and the Queen's are among the loveliest in the world, magnificently set in a Perthshire glen with views of the Ochils on one side and the Grampians on the other. The 13th is known as "Braid's Brawest" after the great James Braid who designed the Gleneagles courses. Your drive has to carry a ridge on which two large bunkers lie at different angles to trap the ball, and having placed that shot perfectly, you then need a long-iron or a second wood meticulously struck to an elevated, far from generous green beset by bunkers. A great four if you can get it.

Killarney, Eire. 18th: 202 yards: par-3
A splendid and picturesque short hole to finish one of Ireland's most glamorous golf courses. You play across a bay of the lough to a green on a peninsula backed by water behind and on the right, and hedged in by trees. You have to be long enough but not too long, dead straight and you also have to stay on the green when you get there. One of the best short holes in the British Isles. Mercifully a massive bank of rhododendrons screens you from the clubhouse.

Moseley, Warwickshire, England. 6th: 396 yards: par-4
This is a remarkable, really challenging hole with all kinds of fascinating problems. To begin with the 396 yards are somewhat illusory. You begin by having to carry a lake of about 100 yards or so in width to a steeply rising fairway which then disappears round a high wood towards the invisible green. Played strictly around the dog-leg the length would be more like 440 yards and you would have to hit a very good drive of well over 200 yards, to get a sight of the green for your second shot. Virtually the only route to par is to carry the wood off the tee, which needs a drive of at least 190 yards clearing 30-foot trees with its dying fall. Then you still have a tricky shot to the green tucked into the side of the hill with a sharp fall away to the left. The big boys aim even nearer the green over the woods but this means a carry of about 230 yards, clearing some gigantic beeches as you come in to land. If you make it, you then have a comparatively simple nine-iron to the green but any way you play it, there are few more satisfying par-fours anywhere.

Two pine trees growing in the centre of the green spell out the number of the hole at Shannon, Grand Bahama.

Vale do Lobo, Algarve, Portugal. 7th: 201 yards: par-3

This is one of the most photographed holes in the world and with justice. It could hardly be more dramatic to look at with its carry from the tee over two sea gorges of rust-red cliffs to a green with a bunker in front and trees behind. The carry is not long – about 150 yards – but the tee shot must be placed with spot-on accuracy because you either have to land on the narrow green and stop or pitch short and hop gently onto the green. With the wind off the sea this can be a really tough hole but it is always a pleasure to play, like the rest of the Vale do Lobo course, one of my particular favourites as much for the warm welcome in the clubhouse from manager David Vansittart as for its beauty and challenge.

Pevero, Costa Smeralda, Sardinia. 4th: 387 yards: par-4

Perhaps the main hazard at this hole is less anything Trent Jones designed than the spectacular view as you stand on the tee looking down the long valley which drops towards the bay, with craggy mountains on each side and purple-blue islands on the distant horizon. But there are also bunkers to right and left in the valley where your drive is likely to finish, and then you must play your second uphill to a narrow hammer-head-shaped plateau green bunkered on the right, with a steep drop to a lake on the left – and the green is treacherously fast.

Estoril, Portugal. 5th: 494 yards: par-5

This course, set between the Sintra mountains and the sea at the fashionable resort near Lisbon, is not long but never lacking in interest. The fifth is fairly straight but the drive has to be in the right place in the narrow tree-lined valley to get your second shot up the steep slope to enable you to play an accurate chip to the well-bunkered green. Placing your drive is the key to this hole. It has to be in the middle on the flat otherwise it is very tricky indeed to get the second shot right.

Shannon, Grand Bahama. 13th: 221 yards: par-3
This is a scenically beautiful and testing hole on the newest of the two fine courses in the Lucayan-Shannon golf complex on one of the world's top golf islands, Grand Bahama. You play from an elevated tee across a valley to a green on the other side with an encroaching lake on the right and trees narrowing the fairway on the left and a really deep, steep bunker just under the green. As if that didn't make things difficult enough there are a couple of pine trees growing in the middle of the green, one straight and one bent, forming the number 13. Gimmicky maybe, but very beautiful and definitely unlucky for some!

Old Course, St. Andrews, Scotland. 1st: 374 yards: par-4
This is not the most difficult hole on the most famous golf course in the world but it is definitely the most nerve-wracking. There you stand on the tee in front of the clubhouse of the Royal and Ancient, the home of golf, where every great player in the world has stood, watched by the beady eyes of the caddies and other implacable assessors of the golf swing hanging over the white fence behind you. There is plenty of fairway to aim at provided you don't slice, but you have to clear the road with your drive to have any hope of getting your second shot over the dreaded Swilcan Burn which runs just in front of the green. The secret is to play out to the left so that you have only one bit of the burn to cross to the green instead of the loop which is your fate if your drive is tucked away on the right. There is plenty of room behind the burn and the green is quite deep, so take one more club than you first thought of. If you have to wade into the Swilcan and retrieve your ball for a penalty of one shot, you will at least have the consolation of knowing that much better players than you have had to do just that on this hole. The first at the Old Course gets into my list because, as the great Bobby Jones once said, "If I had ever been set down in any one place and told I was to play there, and nowhere else for the rest of my life, I should have chosen the Old Course." There is not much I have in common with Bobby Jones, but there is that.

Steady rather than spectacular golf is the keynote of John Garner's game. His selection and subsequent performance in the Ryder Cup match at St. Louis in 1971 drew criticism, which has since been effectively answered by his fine play.

Quiet New Zealander Bob Charles is the most successful left-hander in professional golf history. British Open Champion in 1963 and Piccadilly World Match-Play Champion in 1969 he has been a top money-winner in America for many years.

Practice facilities during an Open Championship at St. Andrews are somewhat restricted and a long way from the R. and A. clubhouse. Many professionals take to the three-mile expanse of smooth sand as soon as the tide turns. Here Tommy Horton puts in a lonely evening session.

Winner of the U.S. Amateur Championship in 1969 and a member of the losing American Walker Cup side at St. Andrews in 1971 Steve Melnyk went on to win the British Amateur in that same year before turning professional.

Brian Huggett, nicknamed the Welsh Bulldog because of his great tenacity and will to win has been a major British tournament winner for 11 years. The Open is the only major British honour he has failed to win.

Johnny Miller, who finished eighth in the U.S. Open when still an amateur, is one of the leading young professionals on the American tour. A consistent money-winner on tour since his 1969 début, he finished second in the U.S. Masters in 1971.

Brian Barnes, one of Britain's most widely travelled competitors, has the distinction of becoming the first British winner of the Australian Wills Masters title in 1970. Consistency is the keynote of his success.

*Chi Chi Rodriguez,
eight and a half stone
Mexican joker, is reputed
to hit the ball a greater
distance pound for pound
than any other professional.
He has recently swapped
his comedy routine for a
more serious attitude to the
game, taking to serious
practice and running five
miles every day to keep fit.*

16

Let's Welcome the Ladies

by Pam Brassington

There was a very fine book written a few years ago called *Black Like Me* by John Howard Griffin, a white American who had his skin darkened and spent quite a long time travelling around the United States as a negro to see what it was like. By and large, he didn't care for the way he was treated.

I, without nearly so much of an effort, have just spent a year heavily disguised as a woman golfer and I don't care for the way *I've* been treated, either. I would like to say straight away that I'm really not a feminist or an aggressive women's liber. I haven't burnt my bra, I don't make militant speeches and up to now I'd have said that there wasn't too much prejudice around between the sexes because all my life I've worked in journalism where pay and working conditions are equal for men and women.

Nobody's ever kicked me out of a works canteen, even I've always been allowed to take my chances in the rissoles and green pea stakes along with everybody else, including printers in inky overalls.

But I put down my pen and take up a beautiful new three-iron, and what happens? I'll tell you – instant humiliation that has nothing to do with the way I actually play golf. I know exactly how artisan members must have felt years ago, when they were allowed to join certain clubs on sufferance at a reduced subscription providing they changed in separate locker rooms, didn't use the bar, and were only allowed on to the course before dawn and after dusk or something equally silly.

Clubs still perpetrate the present-day extension of this kind of inequality. The first time I came across the effects of it was in North London when I went along to watch a competition one winter Saturday and was driven from the course by a torrential rainstorm. Along with about a dozen others I belted for the clubhouse, where we'd been told we were welcome as visitors, and aimed for the first public door I could see. When I fell over the threshold a furious bellow of "Get out – you can't come in here!" stopped me in my tracks. "Mercy me," I thought (or something like it), "I've burst into the men's locker room by mistake, how embarrassing."

Had I? Had I thump! I was in the Men's bar, and if you think I'm exaggerating their reaction to an honest mistake then you still don't understand. They were mad as hatters and actually advanced on me threateningly – honestly they did. I had to go out into the rain again and beat piteously on the Pro's door.

Then there was the occasion a few weeks ago at a posh club in the Midlands, which shall be nameless because my brother-in-law's a member and might be even more embarrassed than he undoubtedly is already. I'd been playing a round with him (if you see what I mean) and afterwards he invited me into the bar for a drink before going home for dinner. At this point I have to tell you what I was wearing: blue trousers, blue tee shirt over red sweater, natty red and white golf hat. Hardly had I grasped my cool half-pint of lager when a large man approached my brother-in-law and mumbled confidentially in his ear. I caught the words: "You do understand, don't you old chap . . . rules . . . not the thing . . . a few big-wigs here tonight," and the next thing I knew I was being hustled into the corridor, to drink between the showcases of silver trophies away from the sight of those I had offended by – wait for it – wearing trousers. Listen, I've lunched at the *Ritz*, in trousers and I've never been anything but welcomed.

I would ask in all seriousness just why golf clubs think they have to be so mindful of segregation and appearance. After all they're basically sports clubs – or have I got it all wrong? Any other such organisation puts the sport part of it first and I really can't see why, provided you're clean and tidy and don't wear spikes, you shouldn't go into the bar wearing what you please. The only other sporting activity in which I take part is skiing, when I get the chance, and if I came down from the slopes and changed into a cocktail dress before going for a drink my fellow skiers would fall about more than usual. The most you do on these occasions is take off your ski boots.

My charges against golf clubs, if I may sound so stern, go further than niggles about what I can wear in the bar provided I'm allowed to enter in the first place. I'm new to golf, as I said, and apart from the fact that I couldn't afford to join a club in the London area even if they'd have me, I gather that my next grumble would be about the women's handicapping system. Its effect, if not its intention, is to make it more difficult for a woman to get a good handicap than for a man – something to do with the number of cards you have to hand in to the handicapping committee.

Yet another grumble would be that I'd have to be a "lady member". I don't want to be labelled a "lady member", just a member. I'm a golfer, not an ambitious orang-outang that doesn't know its limitations. I want to pay my share and be treated without discrimination, as I am in my working life and in most other leisure activities.

Come to think of it, perhaps I am a feminist after all. I watched the Trevor Philpott File on golf on television the other week and I came over all cynical when I heard an English club official say they had vacancies for lady members. All in all, I'm not surprised.

"I tried sharing Fred's hobby, but his golf bag sprained my back."

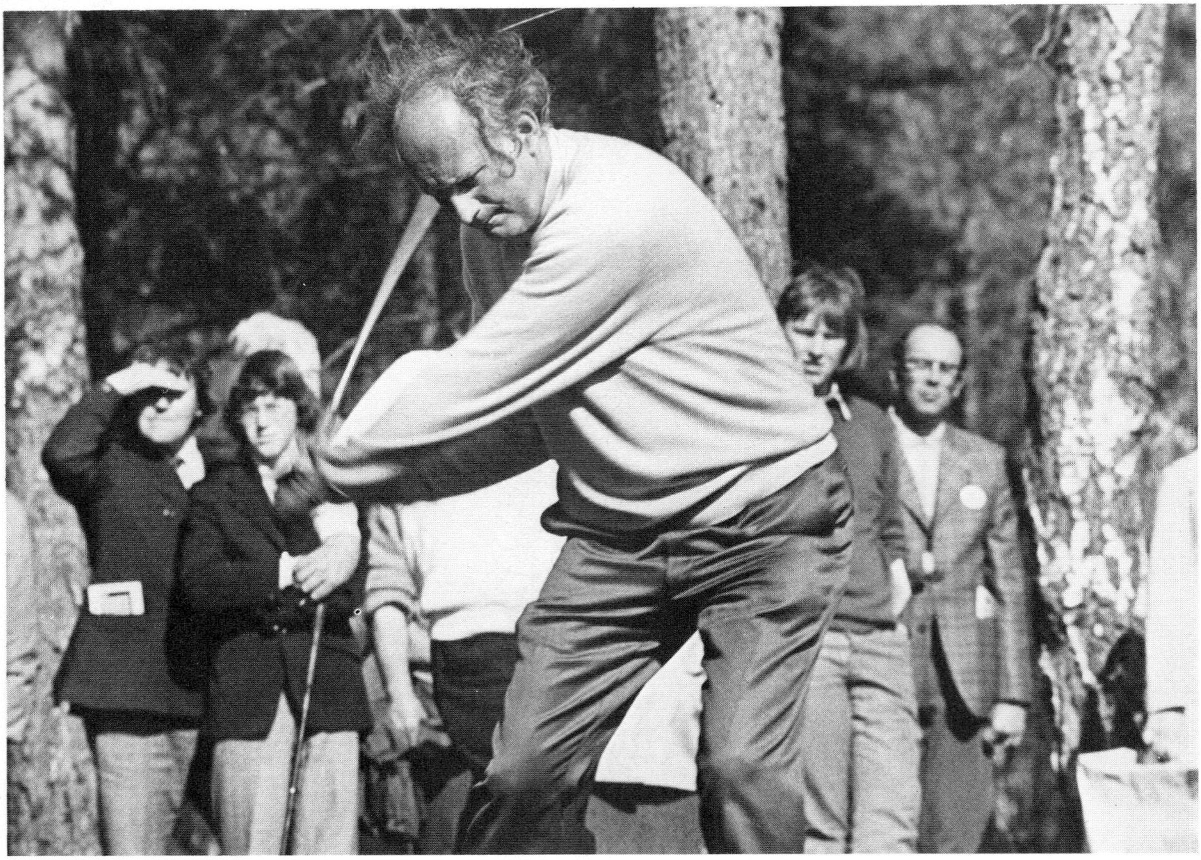

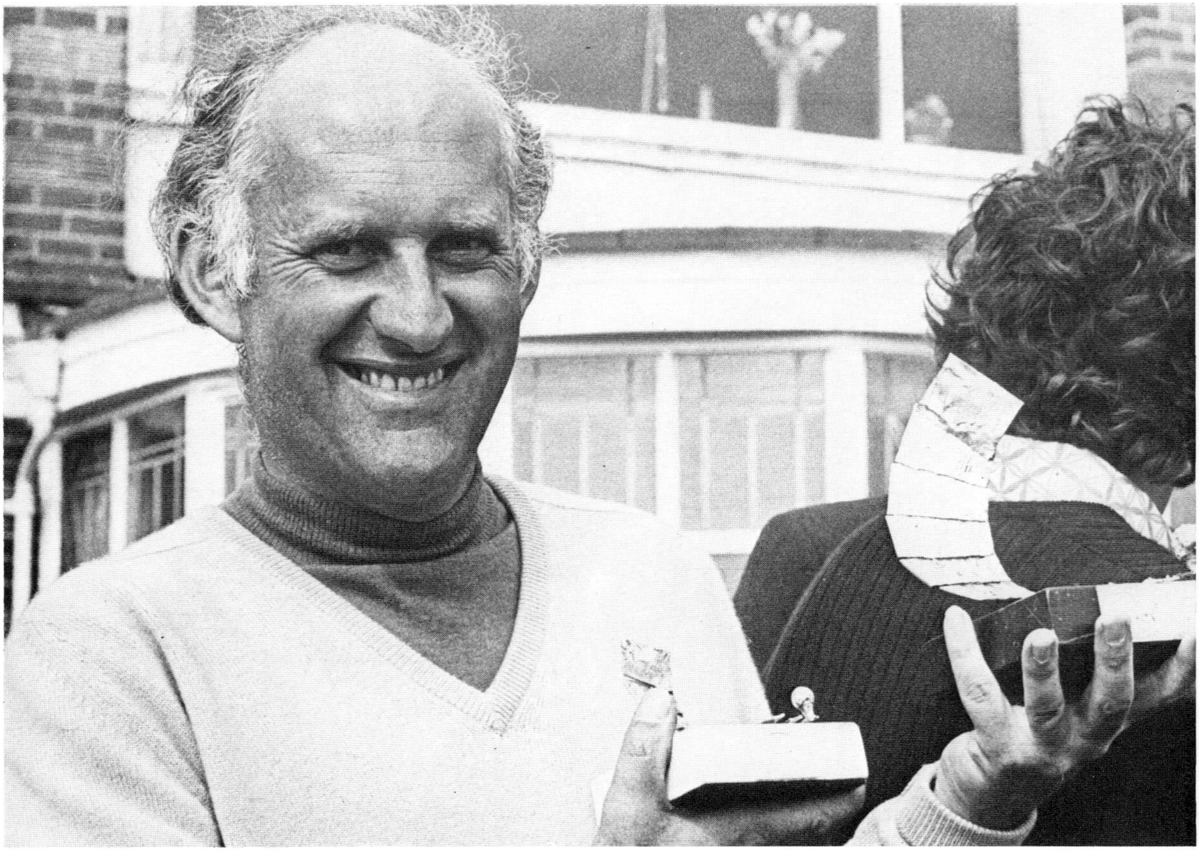

Neil Coles

"To feel right is half the battle in golf. And freezing behind the ball with every muscle tense is a sure preliminary to failure."

"The idea of a glamorous existence amid plaudits of the crowds and the adulation of the golf writers never entered my head and now takes second place to the idea of making a financial success of my chosen calling."

"Walter Hagen wrote that he never wanted to be a millionaire, but only to live like one. Well, I never want to be a millionaire because I shouldn't know how to behave like one."

"One of the reasons I do not do well in the Open is because I dislike seaside courses. I do not think you get as much reward for good shots as you do on inland courses."

"I am one of those outwardly calm types who is actually boiling away quietly inside, although I have never really been tortured by my nerves."

"You cannot afford to think about anything else but playing this game if you want to stay on top. Even when you're not playing you've got to be thinking about it."

18

The Champion Makers

Behind almost every star professional golfer there is a boss-cum-confidant-cum-teacher. In British golf, two of the best-known of these backroom boys are DICK BURTON *and* BILL SHANKLAND. *Both star performers in their own right, these two have steered many top professionals in winning directions – Burton as pro at Coombe Hill, Shankland as pro at Potters Bar.*

Dick Burton relieved Reg Whitcombe of the Open Championship trophy in 1939 and, due to circumstances beyond his control, retained it until 1946.

"They tell me that winning the Open today can make a fellow more than £100,000," says Burton. "I never dwell on it but my victory worked out at 50 quid a year. And the fact that I was the holder had no effect on the bloke who handed out the wages on payday. I think I started at two bob a day."

Burton, famed these days as the mentor of men like Neil Coles, Jimmy Hitchcock, Ken Bousfield and Craig Defoy, was 32 when he ran a niblick shot to within eight yards and holed the putt for a three to beat Chicago's Johnny Bulla by two shots.

Those days have long gone and Burton now finds peace and considerable renown as Coombe Hill pro and long-time guide to future stars. As he says: "I have been blessed with good health and the best job in the world. In golf you meet nice people who are out relaxing away from their jobs. The game breeds nice people and I have been lucky enough to meet thousands of them. What more can a man ask?"

The touring pros of Burton's early days were far removed from the jet-set millionaires of modern golf. His companions were Bill Davies of Wallasey and Jimmy Adams. Davies played the role which Burton himself now takes with his string of successful assistants at Coombe Hill.

"He was the pioneer of charting courses although he did not carry around pencil and paper the way Nicklaus and the others do today. When I practised with him before a tournament he would make me play three balls for the second shot. That way, hitting the shots in from distances varying by 40

Dick Burton

yards, he reckoned that I could cope with any weather conditions which might crop up when the tournament began.

"We never putted out when we got to the green. Bill argued that in practice the pins were always towards the front of the green, so we aimed at where we thought the pins would be later. His theory was that to three-putt or even worse in practice would create some psychological block when playing the hole for real. So we usually hit our seconds to the back of the greens, rolled along a putt or two at the imaginary hole and went off to the next tee. I have always felt that too many good players leave their good putting behind in practice.

"Bill would tell me never to add up what I took and boast about a 66. It was tomorrow that counted. Watch Neil Coles today getting ready for a tournament. He never gets himself worked up about missing putts

the day before. I don't think he even counts his score.

"Neil must be one of the best players in the world. It is impossible to say what he would have done had he gone for the moon in the way that Jacklin and some of the others have done. He has such amazing control of himself. I have known him since he started and have never seen him lose this wonderful calm.

"He is a very good driver and certainly hits it long enough to succeed on those big American courses. But Neil would never be happy leading the life the really big boys are forced to lead. He will never be one of the jet set and it is not solely because he dislikes flying. He is not built the way Jacklin and Player and the others are. But I rate him just as good a player."

Burton believes that Ken Bousfield never hit long enough to reach world class. "But

137

within 100 yards of the hole I have never seen anyone better."

Jimmy Hitchcock disappointed him. "He had tremendous natural talent and I thought he would have been one of the greats. But he is always too fidgety, always picking up imaginary bits of stuff on the green, never settled mentally like Coles."

He feels the same about Tony Grubb. "Tony is a great mover but too often slips in a few bad holes."

The latest on the Coombe Hill assembly line is American-born Craig Defoy. "I think we may have a real one in Craig. He is a very good striker and has the perfect build. Unlike Coles he will go anywhere. He is far from a good chipper but I think this will come."

If Burton is famed for his guidance of a host of top professionals, former Potters Bar professional Bill Shankland can claim renown for the way he steered Tony Jacklin to greatness.

Shankland, a dominant figure in Australian Rugby League circles before settling in England in 1930, has early claims to fame in his own right. He was a Rugby League cup finalist at Wembley three times with Warrington, finished joint third behind Burton in the 1939 Open, fourth behind Fred Daly in 1947 and joint sixth behind Max Faulkner in 1951.

Latterly, however, he has been the man to knock the rough edges off Jacklin who was 17 when he first went to Shankland at Potters Bar.

"I had three good assistants, John Sharkey, Alan Gillies and Colin Christison who have since done well as club pros. Jacklin came down from Lincolnshire with some sort of reputation as a good player but it didn't impress me.

"I recognised that the kid had guts, but

he had a terrible palm grip with his left hand and was soon losing 10 bob to the other three lads. Although the new boy he was always throwing out challenges, but it was not until he had lost most of his pay for the first month that he asked me to have a look at his grip and swing. That left-hand position caused him to fade almost every shot. He was swinging from in-to-out with a flat shoulder action and although it took him quite a while to ask for advice he learned quickly when it was given and he was soon taking money from the others.

"He needed daily practice and I gave him the time for it. He hated working in the shop but did his fair share. It would have been crazy at that time to treat him any differently from the others, although I realised that he was something special. There was always something about him, an inner conviction which he had which spread to me after I had known him for a while.

"I remember him playing in front of me in the Middlesex championship in 1962. At the 14th he shanked one out of bounds and took seven. He then finished with three threes and a four. I thought then that the kid had guts."

A year earlier the generous Potters Bar members had wanted to send Jacklin to South Africa. "I knew that Snead had played Locke out there in a nine-match series and lost the lot. I knew all about the greens and felt sure that Tony was not ready to tackle them. The members thought I was being hard on him and the kid was disappointed but I was then, and still am now, all against youngsters chasing round the world before they are ready to bring credit to both themselves and their country. He went the next year and won nothing, but the swing was almost there.

"By 1967 he had shown enough on the

circuit to suggest he was ready for anything. There was a disaster at Stoke Poges that year when he finished with a six at the short 16th, an eight at the 17th after a cracking drive and a six at the 18th. He came to me, almost in tears, the next morning and asked me to have a look at his swing. For a week we went out for two hours a day and soon after he won the Pringle. Once he had made the breakthrough I was sure nothing could stop him.

"He has changed his method considerably – using leg power much more. He is a wonderful driver and bunker player and when in the right seam one of the world's best putters. I suppose I am biased but he is hard enough and good enough to stay at the top for another 15 years."

Bill Shankland

19 America v. Britain:
The Club Golf Scene

The British club golfer has less in common with his American cousin than do our tournament professionals or top amateurs with their U.S. contemporaries. The supreme difference between everyday golf in the two countries is cost. Golf in Britain is extraordinarily cheap. In fact, for the man or woman who plays frequently at a modest club, but who does not socialise heavily, on a cost-per-hour basis it has to be one of the cheapest of all mass-participant sports. Viewed any way you like in America, golf is extremely expensive. In fact, for the person who joins a private club only to play golf, but cannot do so more than once a week, it is one of the most expensive of all popular American pastimes.

A few figures drive home the point. In Britain, the highest club subscriptions today, after much recent inflation, are around £80 at the top London clubs, and the lowest for which full membership benefits are available are probably about £12 at a few of the smaller Scottish and Irish clubs. A mean average for the whole country would perhaps be £30. In America, top subscriptions can be \$10,000 (£4,000) and the lowest at small private clubs with only nine-hole courses can be as much as \$500 or £200. It is certainly true that, around the major cities, an income of not less than \$30,000 (£12,000) is needed before a family man can afford membership of a "good" club. There are some "name" establishments where his application wouldn't be considered unless he was making probably twice that sum.

Rates of pay and living costs in the States are, of course, very different from those of Britain. But the huge difference in the relative basic cost of golf is inescapable whichever way you look at everyman's version of the game in the two countries. Assuming the British club golfer pays a £30

subscription, plays 80 times a year and takes three hours a round, his sport is costing him just over 12p an hour. If \$1,000 is an average U.S. subscription, an American playing the same amount at the same speed would be paying nearly 20 times as much. No wonder he likes to stretch a round out to five or six hours!

Nor are basic subscriptions the only area in which the cost of American golf exceeds ours. Club entry fees are usually at least the equivalent of a year's subscription and golf equipment is between 30 and 60 per cent more costly, depending at which end of the market you shop. At many clubs members are expected to spend a regular minimum on food and drink, and sometimes are billed for it even if they haven't consumed a crumb. And, of course, at many clubs you're not allowed to play without a caddie. But the real twist of the knife in the wound comes when a club happens to make a loss on its year's workings. The American solution to this not-unheard-of problem in Britain is beautifully simple. The deficit is divided by the number of members, and everybody gets a nice little New Year surprise.

Two questions might well occur to British golfers who've never actually seen an American club. First, how can so many people – 12,750,000 is the currently quoted figure – afford to play? Second, how have they managed to make the game so wildly expensive?

Most of the answer to number one is, of course, tied up with the comparative fiscal standards of the two nations: middle-class Americans simply have more spending power than middle-class Britons, especially after tax. There is also the point that a great many American golfers never get beyond the "publinxes" or public courses, which, though not cheap by our standards, are within the

Luckily not all British golf clubs are as outdated as this locker room at a South Coast club would indicate.

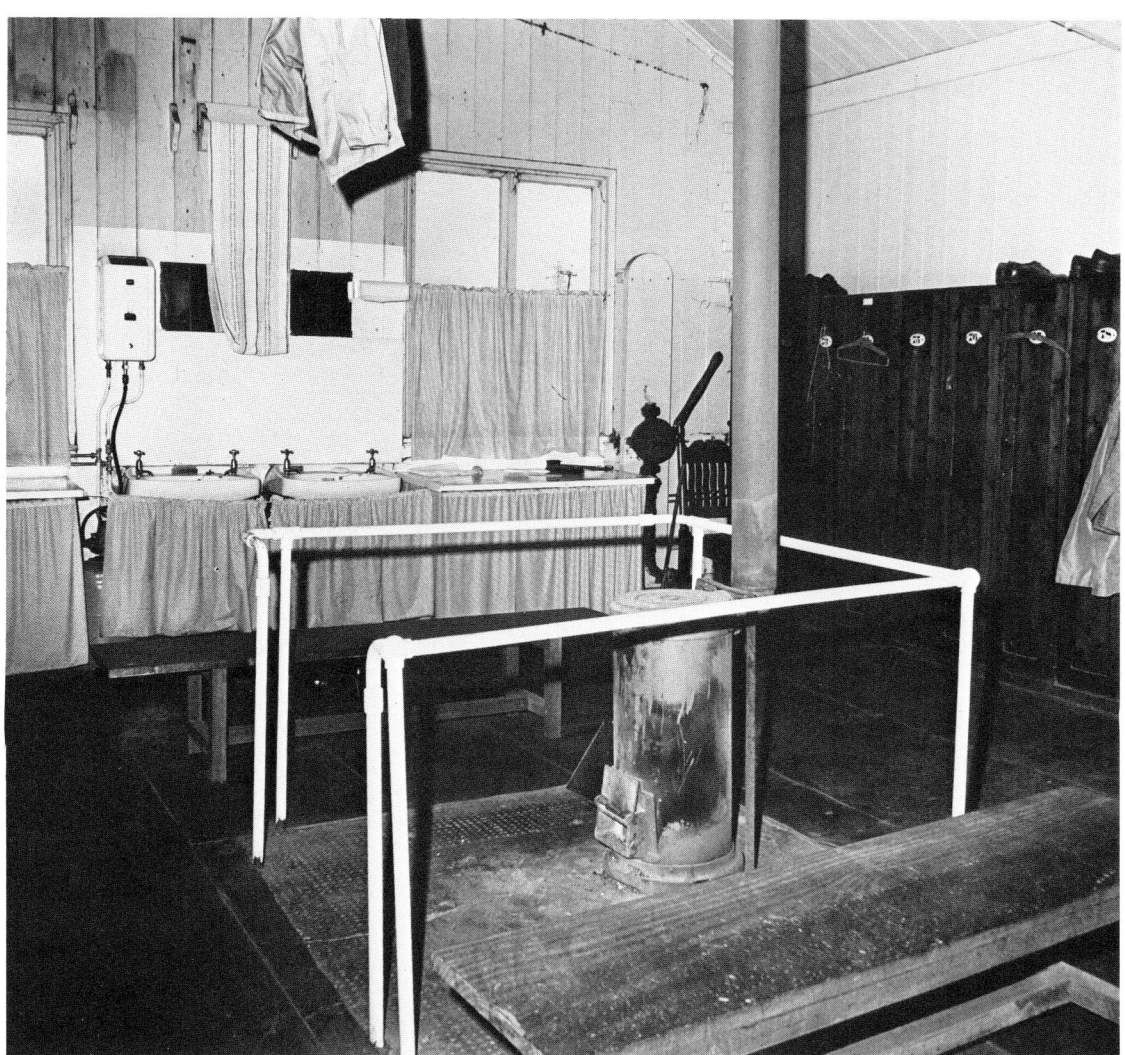

reach of most wage-earners. But a not in-significant factor beyond these is the provision of club membership as a career perk, especially at the top executive level. A great many Americans play golf largely at their company's expense. In fact, so common is this "fringe benefit" in the big cities that company rank is often the chief determining factor in obtaining club membership. It is by

no means uncommon for a man to be persuaded into a new job by the carrot of membership of a select club, or himself to seek berths that promise escalation up the country-club scale. As a result, you often don't get the same degree of social mix in U.S. club life as has latterly liberalised and expanded the British game. Equality of status, especially financial status, among the

members is a noticeable trait of many U.S. clubs; and a golfer's club can be much more a badge of career rank or wealth than a measure of his playing skill or even his enthusiasm for the game.

This situation obviously supplies part of the answer to question two, how Americans have managed to make golf so expensive. The game is often so tightly meshed with commerce that it develops deep sociological connotations in a land where vocational achievement and wealth are the prime yardsticks of human endeavour and status. But the two principal cost factors, it has always seemed to me, are of a strictly material nature, namely the type of golf course which it has been necessary to develop to satisfy the American concept of the game; and the country-club system that, by force of America's size, climate, love of community life and addiction to outdoor activity, has

grown up around the ancient Scots' simple, even spartan, pastime.

For Americans golf is essentially a game of man against course, of "shooting a score". Because of this attitude, their courses have swung away from the simple naturalistic British style to more artificiality, standardisation and rigid control of playing conditions. Whether or not you favour this type of sophisticated golf (and most of the world outside Britain does), such courses are extremely expensive to build and even more costly to run. The less rough you have on a golf course, the more sand; and the harder the bashing you give fairways, tees and greens by keeping them soggy, the more machinery, materials and men you need to maintain it. Almost all U.S. private club courses are roughless, stuffed with sand and heavily watered. The size of the outdoor staffs and the budgets for materials and

Even classic courses such as Troon (left, site of the 1973 Open Championship) and Rye (right) have clubhouses which are far from lavish, although Troon's clubhouse has been extended since this picture was taken.

machinery needed to keep them in peak condition, would turn any British greenkeeper emerald with envy. They would also, without doubt, turn any British club committee grey with horror.

But these are relatively minor factors in the cost of American golf. The single biggest factor of all is that private golf clubs in the States are not golf clubs at all – at least, not what we know as golf clubs, i.e. places to which you rush, change your shoes, sprint round the course, rinse your hands, have a quick drink or two, then dash away to do something else somewhere else. They are country clubs in the fullest possible sense of that phrase: recreational complexes-cum-community centres designed to serve the wide-ranging sporting, social and even cultural needs of the whole family.

In America, a golf course may be the focal point of activity for a large proportion of members, but it is almost always just one of a club's facilities. A swimming-pool is a virtually standard attachment, and sometimes there are two, or a children's pool. Tennis is almost equally common, and if anybody ever made a census throughout the country they would probably find within a few yards of a golf course amenities for almost every participant sport yet invented – shooting, hunting, fishing, riding, sailing, skiing, squash, curling, basketball – you name it, somebody's got it. And it is all this, of course, not golf alone, that costs the money.

The fact is, however, that most Americans

143

– even those to whom the game of golf is life itself – happily accept, even welcome, such a state of affairs. With all this to hand virtually on their doorsteps, and in most parts of the country a climate that for many months stimulates an already highly developed enjoyment of outdoor life, the country club has become for them, keen golfers or otherwise, virtually a second home, an integral part of life, as important as a motor car or a deep freeze. It's like having your own high-class holiday camp just over the back fence. A man's subscription usually covers his wife and children, or they come in at nominal rates. Clubhouses are built, run and staffed to provide, normally in a very high degree of comfort, almost round-the-clock services for large groups of people with varying tastes and doing different things. Then there is the social life, formal and informal: full and intense and immensely

satisfying to an instinctively "neighbourly" people.

Having experienced it all, one isn't in the least surprised to find that many Americans – wives and children as well as addicted golfers – spend more time at "the club" than they do in their own homes. And, of course, when you weigh up what they are getting, it becomes easier to understand – and, if you had to, perhaps even accept – the high cost. After all, members of active British families probably fill their free time doing more or less what Americans do, except that they have to go to lots of different places in the process, which enables them to avoid looking at the cost of their leisure as a total. If they did, they might be in for a shock.

In what other ways does U.S. club golf differs from ours? There are many. To begin with, except in those southern States where it is always summer, golf is largely a seasonal

The magnificent Old Warson Country Club at St. Louis, Missouri, where the Ryder Cup match was played in 1971, demonstrates the opulence of many American clubs. The courses in America also tend to be man-made while their British equivalents are shaped by nature.

game in America. Most people pack up at the first sign of winter and don't resume until well into spring, even if the weather facilitates play. It has always seemed paradoxical how most Americans think nothing of playing in heat and humidity that would melt the enthusiasm of even the nuttiest British addict, and yet would not dream of swinging a club in the chill, damp and breezy conditions we regard as "ideal for golf". The fact is, I suppose, that they have a choice and we don't. If weather controlled your golf in Britain, you'd rarely play.

Because of the country-club environment,

their fine-weather approach, and the influences of pro tournament golf, as well as their natural love of colour, Americans like to dress up for golf, whereas traditionally we have tended to dress down. Indeed, so far as equipment and haberdashery go, most U.S. club golfers might well be last week's $50,000 winner hot off the tour. Two years is the average life of a set of golf clubs in the States, as against seven in Britain. Enormous bags, fancy head-covers, multi-hued shoes, funny hats and the generally stylish and strikingly coloured raiment of the U.S. golfing male often shocks the conservative Briton at first sight. But you soon get used to it, because the whole American golfing scene is somehow so much lighter, brighter and more vivacious (used to it all, that is, except Bermuda shorts, surely the most unflattering creation in the history of the rag trade, especially to men).

One aspect of American club golf that has

long been notorious is its pace. To Britons, the speed of a round is as important as the score it produces, often more so in club life. Anything over three hours for a single or three and a half for a four-ball seems to produce in many people the same sort of sensations – and reactions – as would slow strangulation. By this criteria, Americans do play golf infernally slowly, and, in fact, the problem has become so bad that various U.S. authorities are trying to do something about it. Five and a half hours a round is common.

What produces this lethargy? One answer is heat, or rather humidity. When the atmosphere is like a sauna bath, as it often is in summer in many parts of the States, you don't feel like tilting at Olympic records. Another is the predilection for stroke-play, compounded by endless gambling permutations. Everybody has to go on hitting it until it goes in the hole, whether it takes 3 or 33. Yet another factor is television. Americans are eager and quick to ape the successful in any sphere, hence the interminable deliberations and perambulations of tournament professionals as shown on television are reproduced, often perhaps unconsciously, at club level.

But the main reason is more basic than these: "What", ask the Americans, "is the hurry? We're not going any place else. We're here all day, and whatever time we come in we can get a drink in the locker room and eat in the grill room. Also, I enjoy playing golf, so why should I be in a hurry to get it over? Take your time and enjoy yourself!"

The fact is that the time-scale of American golf, like so many other factors, derives at root from the country-club set-up. It's just a nice place to be. If you don't have any work to do, are not planning a trip any place, it

has all you want for your physical amusement, inner needs and social delectation. Here, perhaps, lies the one antidote to the hectic pace of life generally in America.

In Britain, four-ball match-play is the most popular form of club golf, but there is still a good deal of foursome and singles play, again almost always on the match basis. The only time we count all the strokes and write them down is during medal competition, a style of golf that up to three-quarters of the membership of many clubs very rarely, if ever, indulge in. Consequently, despite the well-meant and energetic efforts of various authorities, handicaps in Britain are largely fictional, or at best a sign of what a golfer once did in his prime or might, with a miracle, do in the future. In American club golf, foursomes play is virtually unknown, match-play rare, and singles go out usually only when it is impossible to make a four. The name of the U.S. game is fourball stroke-play, with everything holed out and written down, and followed by a long session over cold drinks in locker rooms sorting out the bets, which usually sound terrifyingly complicated to a non-initiate. Whatever drawbacks this format may seem to have by our philosophy, it has one great advantage. Everybody can be accurately handicapped according to current form.

There isn't space here to go into the mathematics of U.S. handicapping systems, except to say that they are extremely rational and that they work (often these days with the aid of computers). What is worth bearing in mind, against the next time you play with an American is that if he says he is 7, or 17 or 27, given reasonable conditions that is what he is almost certain to play to.

However, accurately as the Americans measure their form, they have in the main little cause to be proud of it. It is only the top tournament pros and amateurs, an élite band of maybe 500 players, who are perhaps better than their British counterparts. Club for club throughout the two nations, Britain's weekend golfers could win every time, especially under their own course and weather conditions. A simple comparison of upper handicap limits and scoring attitudes makes this point. In Britain 24 is the top mark, and it is in effect a mark of shame, off which even the least committed novice is anxious to move as fast as possible. If you can't break 100, the general consensus of opinion is that you can't play. In the States men's handicaps go up to 40, and it is not unusual to hear a golfer say, with some pride, that today he "shot just a couple over the 100". (The classic remark of all time came from the golfer who is reputed to have said, absolutely seriously, when asked how he was getting on: "Man, I'm getting real hot! Why, I've been pooping it round there regular in the low 120s.")

When you consider that U.S. courses are, in the main, very much easier for the club golfer than ours, that most play is in fair weather, and that a very high percentage of Americans play "winter rules" (improving the lie) all the time, it becomes evident that the British club golfer, at least, is entitled to hold his head high.

Why are U.S. playing standards sometimes so poor at the club level? Again the answer rests chiefly in the U.S. country-club set-up. In Britain, a golf club is a golf club, which there is absolutely no point in joining other than to play golf. Generally speaking, being a golf-club member procures no advantages in life's race other than those inherent in the quality of one's course and the camaraderie of one's like-minded fellows. In the States country-club membership is vocationally and socially meaningful, in addition to its much broader value in terms of the recreational fulfilment of the whole family. Hence, you have commonly a situation where people join a club first, then take up golf as an afterthought. Sometimes they become avid enough to strive to play well, but in many cases they golf casually and sporadically as one of a number of lightly followed pursuits that the club happens to make available. This may be excellent for the national health, but it doesn't breed expertise.

For all these reasons and many more, therefore, golf in America is not in the practical sense very much like the British game. But it would be unfair not to mention the areas where the transatlantic cousins have a great deal in common, and, as the two major golfing nations, seemingly always will have.

The American game, like the British game, is full of golf widows, and uncut lawns, and empty office desks. It produces blisters, and slipped discs, and sore feet, and getting up too early and staying out too late. On both sides of the ocean people pore endlessly over golf books, posture in front of mirrors, change clubs, collect putters, bore each other in bars, live for the weekends, don't practise, take brassies out of bunkers, stab two-foot putts, drink one too many, slice, curse and derive divine inspiration from one absolutely solid, perfectly hit shot out of every two hundred.

In other words, although we go about it very differently, the appeal of the game is the same, and so are its frustrations and pleasures, its irritations and benefits. Above all, inexorably linking the two countries is a bond of friendship, tolerance, hospitality and understanding found today, perhaps, only among golfers.

It makes many of the differences of very little moment.

20 Golf's Secret

Thoughts are Best

by George Houghton

Those of us with breasts in which hope springs eternal are more completely involved, and rewarded, than those who have no capacity for optimism. This is the under-surface aspect of golf. The important, pleasurable part.

A golfer who says to himself it is absolutely impossible for him ever to go round the course in par figures is declaring bankruptcy of hope. Average players can remember that on some occasion or other at any hole they have registered a par. That being so, is it not possible to play them all that way – consecutively? Improbable, maybe. But not impossible.

I am told that positive thinking makes champions. Maybe, but some of us don't want to be champions. It is more important to remember that these mental gymnastics increase golf's enjoyment spells of two or three hours of hit and walk into days and nights of ecstasy.

In this think area, amateurs are more favoured than professionals; cubs are luckier than tigers; you-and-I players come out best. Our investment in golf is cash and anguish, but the return is greater for us than for the other fellow, even allowing for the hardware in his trophy cabinet.

After years of asking myself why I bother, it now becomes clear that golf's greatest reward is not superior performance. A sound repetitive swing in the square method is a pain in the neck. Secret thoughts are what really count.

A senior Hertfordshire golfer named Bobby Fox, who illustrated his point by occasional club-flinging, used to say that maximum pleasure only results from total acceptance of golf's love-hate relationship. He believed that the player who doesn't honestly think that some outside agency (such as a bird) is responsible for every bad shot he makes, will never fully appreciate playing a good 'un.

Archie Compston, another cheery cynic, said that happy golf is nine-tenths in the mind. He is quoted: "Next to sunburn, a visit to the dentist, or a wasp sting on the privates, nothing gives a man more masochistic satisfaction than a round of golf."

So much penetrating analysis has gone into golf instruction – professors now explain the varying functions of finger-joints! – that it is soothing relief to remember we can still enjoy homely hates. Maybe our opponent will try out something the pro told him, and lose a few quick holes. . . . This mind-golf can be most satisfying.

The scientific aspect can be a bore. Whether we realise it or not, the various shades of emotional turmoil raise the game to something spiritual and satisfying. Given the right mental capacity, even the finger tingle that comes when you club hard ground can be likened to a sensation in the throat after gulping fine brandy.

To purists, the idea of golf being fun is obnoxious, sacrilegious, and to be deplored. They fall into line with the P. G. Wodehouse character who, when giving advice to a girl, told her never to trust a man who laughs on a golf course. I would go along with that. I don't want golfers to laugh. I want them to be thoroughly sensitive, and enjoy the aspects of our game which are only remotely connected with ball bashing.

I urge boundless hope. Any player can beat his handicap, or any other player, but he must remember that golf can never be beaten. Like the Chinese, you can say – when rape is inevitable, relax and enjoy it. Golf emotions are special. Fully indulged they are the real golf secret.

Although you must expect that some day, somewhere, someone may give you the trick which makes golf easy, this will only help you to play better. Your pleasure won't be increased because performance and pleasure are seldom related. A player is happy after a good round, but if golf's emotion traffic is running smoothly he should be pleasure-saturated anyway.

I have been gently reprimanding a friend who was saddened by the news that Tony Hoyles, 30 days short of his 12th birthday, three inches less than five feet, and three ounces under six stones had, for the second consecutive month, won the Medal competition at West Hove Golf Club. In fewer weeks he reduced his handicap by seven shots. . . . With never a golf lesson in his life.

"This is ridiculous!" said my friend. But golf is like that.

Matt Rimmer is a Briton who started judo, yoga and karate in the United States to keep himself amused while separated from his wife and boy. So much did his health and outlook improve, that on return to his home in Southport he got his 17-year-old son interested. One day, during a visit to the Aintree Driving Range, golf also cropped up. Result: within one year, young John Rimmer is regularly scoring in the low 70s. The Southport professional who has him in hand, is staggered, although uncertain about father Rimmer's winning golf formula:

Judo – to produce overwhelming fitness and confidence.

Karate – to give the killer-instinct.

Yoga – to make the mind calm and control temptations.

Time stumbles on, and the right kind of golf is unchanged and unchangeable. Yet, it is interesting to remember that whatever the teaching pros say, one way to succeed at golf is to gain a judo black belt, be a Dan at karate and practise yoga by sitting on the clubhouse steps contemplating your navel.

Golf is so much to think about. A keen old senior died. The family gathered in the solicitor's office to hear the Will. "And to my niece Sandra I leave my faithful old putter. . . ." There were sniggers, until the vultures discovered that the wealthy old golf addict's putter was gold-plated and inset with two rubies and six diamonds. The delightful weapon must have given the old man infinite pleasure, not so much when he used it to tap the ball, but just remembering that he owned such a club. A good example of golf's fringe benefits on the mental side.

Pot and cheque hunters can be so consumed with golf practice and effort that I love to see the physical aspect gently debunked. There was the commercial traveller who always had a putter among his samples so that he could practise in his hotel room. Gary Player has a weighted, short-shafted

150

club for indoor swinging; Frank Stranahan travels with dumb-bells. An American pro caused much upset on arrival at a hotel because he had a shallow box of sand. Everyone supposed it was for practising explosion bunker shots – until they discovered it was for his wife's dog.

People now take to golf like ducks to other ducks during mating season. Which reminds us that so far Russia has not entered this area of enlightenment. If only they could get involved! Strange they never have, even before organised communism.

Bob Randall, once pro at Herne Bay, tried to get Russia golf-minded 60 years ago. I have just seen an old letter which he sent to a friend at the South Beds club. Helped by 26 Russian peasants, Bob made a nine-hole course near St. Petersburg. "My members," he writes, "consisted of a few princes and various consuls. In committee the question came up who should open the course. I suggested the Grand Duke Michael. . . ." Within two years Bob received notification that owing to lack of interest the club had been abandoned.

There has been a borsch-like sourness about Russia's attitude to golf. The present leaders say "a decadent game for English Lords and American millionaires"; "a caste-perpetrating device"; "bourgeoise nonsense"; "a game in which the rich dawdle about and use child labour to carry the heavy implements . . .". Yet, we now learn that the game is being seriously considered by a group of Russian tennis players who have seen what they call "goof" played in Western Europe. They believe the game is a natural for their mild-weather area, near the Black Sea. A lay-out at Souchi is being considered; that is where the big Soviet shots take vacations. Another site is near Yalta. Golf in Russia may well be standing nervously on the bank, about to take the plunge at long last.

Now, comes the 64-rouble question. Will Russians make good golfers? Some say no, because their fingers are too stubby. What rot!

This, you will agree, is where we came in. The "fingers" bit clearly comes from a British or American golf professional. Does it matter what Russian fingers are like, or whether they play well or not?

The important point is – *have communists the capacity for enjoying the think aspect of golf?*

21

Swing the Clubhead

by Ken Adwick

I have always believed that the golf swing should be treated as one overall swinging movement and not as a series of smaller, related actions. If the golfer will only concentrate on swinging the clubhead correctly, then the body, arm, shoulder and leg actions will fall automatically into place.

Having said that, it is nevertheless necessary to have a clear idea of the basics of the swing, and to this end we can break the golf swing down into five parts –

(1) By turning the left shoulder under the chin and keeping both arms straight, yet relaxed, take the club back to roughly waist high.

(2) From this position break the wrists, at the same time turning a little more, and you have then completed the back swing. Naturally, the right arm will bend at this point.

(3) Bring the clubhead back to the ball. You should now be in the same position as when you started.

(4) From this point allow the right shoulder to come under the chin.

(5) At about waist high break the wrists once more, at the same time increasing the turn. Now, in theory, you have reached a position that can be compared with a left-handed player's backswing.

There in its simplest form is the theory of the movement of a golf club and the rock-bottom principles which must be kept in mind at all times.

These five movements are the simplest way of starting off a beginner. Theory is one thing, but what about the important practical side. The golf swing is a swing and must be as smooth and rhythmical as that of the pendulum of a clock swinging backwards and forwards.

In fact, a clock with its swinging pendulum is the best example I know for describing a golf swing. If we imagine that our body, like the clock standing on the mantelshelf, is stationary, our arms and club become the pendulum swinging to and fro.

As the pendulum moves, the bottom of the arc will swing over the same spot each time. But if as the pendulum moves to the right you move the body of the clock one inch in the same direction, then the bottom of the arc of the pendulum will be one inch from its

Think of the golf swing in terms of a giant wheel and you are half-way to adopting the all-important swinging swing. Think of the head as the hub of a wheel and concentrate on swinging the clubhead round the rim on the backswing and through swing.

original position. If you reverse the procedure – as the pendulum moves to the left the clock is moved in the same direction – then the bottom of the arc will be one inch in front of where it was originally.

It follows from this that throughout the swinging of the club your body must remain perfectly still with only the clubhead, hands and arms moving.

Unlike the pendulum we cannot swing on an upright plane because we are bending over. This means that we swing on an inclined plane both on the backswing and also the follow through.

Again, unlike the clock we have to swing the clubhead further back and through than a pendulum travels, so naturally we have to allow our bodies to turn on both the back and forward swing. But I must repeat, the feeling is always that of a clock pendulum swinging to and fro in a smooth and graceful movement.

Now we have to consider the arc and direction in which the clubhead must be swung. I have already explained that this must be on an inclined plane. So let us imagine that we are addressing the ball, that the head is the hub of a wheel with the rim of the wheel placed around us on an inclined plane and that the rim of the wheel is grooved to allow the clubhead to follow that groove throughout the back and forward swing. This will keep the clubhead on an even inclined path.

Poor control of the club by the hands leads to an inconsistent swing path as if the club were following the rim of a buckled wheel. The ungainly body movements which become apparent in such a swing are not the cause of the bad action, but in turn are caused by poor control of the club by the hands.

However, should the clubhead leave the grooved rim then the path of the club will look like that of a buckled wheel.

As the club is controlled only by the hands, all other movements in the golf swing are led by and responsive to the action of the hands. For example, on the crooked wheel illustration it appears that the right shoulder has turned into the shot too soon. This, in fact, is not the cause. The hands have played a very poor part by not following the wheel rim, causing the right shoulder to be thrown out. The right shoulder is only following the lead given by the hands. If the player had kept the club going in that groove by correct hand application then the shoulders would have played their own part and followed the clubhead on the correct path.

The only other thing I have to add to this picture of the wheel is that you must "see" the wheel to be tilted slightly to the right of the target. This will give the so essential slightly inside to out path of the swing.

I am always stressing that hands are the governing factor in the golf swing, and to my mind the greatest of all teachers, the late Ernest Jones, said: "When you swing anything the swinging motion will cause something to bend. Take the motion of opening or closing a door. Your hands are the medium through which you turn the door knob and push or pull the door. The hinges give in response to the power used through your hands, there is no initiative action of the hinge.

"You don't make movement to move the clubhead, you move the clubhead to make movement."

That needs a little explaining. There are three vital points: the brain, the clubhead, and the medium between them, the hands. It is the hands that hold the club and they are the only way that you can transmit to the clubhead the power you wish to deliver to the ball.

If you think of the clubhead and the direction in which you wish it to be swung, then the various parts of your body must respond naturally to the path the clubhead takes.

If you have a bad swing then the moving parts of your body will look and seem awkward. The onlooker will say that you did this, or that with your arms or legs. Quite right. But it goes deeper. All he is seeing is the response to a poor swing. Put the swing right and the body movements change, too, since they are followers and not leaders.

The power of your body is applied through the hands and, just like the door hinges, your body will respond. The body, like a dynamo, generates and supplies the power. The hands are like the electric wires which deliver that power. However, if the hands are weak in comparison with the rest of the body, they can be compared with a resistance in an electrical circuit, reducing the power being supplied.

Within the swing there must be a strike. A poor player who heaves at the ball is using the club more like a lever and there is no striking force in levering anything. It is the strike within a swing that we are endeavouring to achieve. We want a striking blow rather than a levering or pushing action. Let me pass on a simple example. You push in a

drawing pin. This is a form of applied power. But when you drive in a nail with a hammer you are using power delivered by striking. This is exactly what is needed in the swinging of a golf club.

I am not asking you to force your swing. If you do you turn the swing into a lever. What we are seeking is gradually increased speed at impact – resulting in a swinging strike. The poor golfer always looks as if he is straining in every muscle and in fact putting a lot of unnecessary effort into the movement. There is no clubhead speed in this, only waste of energy. Take the player who is a regular "heaver". There comes a time when he wants to play a shot short of trouble. He decides in his mind he will use an easy swing – and the usual result is that the ball travels further than intended and into the trouble which he tried to avoid. This is because he has swung instead of heaved and gained greater clubhead speed at impact as a result.

I try to avoid the word "hitting" when talking about golf. To my mind there is a difference between "hitting" and "striking" The way I see it is that in "hitting" you are using uncontrolled brute force in the golf swing, whereas with "striking" the image is of power delivered through swinging and allied with timing.

Nor do I like using the word "grip", although it is hard to avoid. The word I really prefer is "hold". You don't "grip" a pen, you "hold" it. The word "grip" is associated with a vice-like intensity which stifles any freedom of movement. And freedom of movement is our ultimate aim.

Remember the pendulum action and its smoothness, have another look at the wheel with its inclined plane, and seek that sweet and powerful strike within an uninterrupted swing.

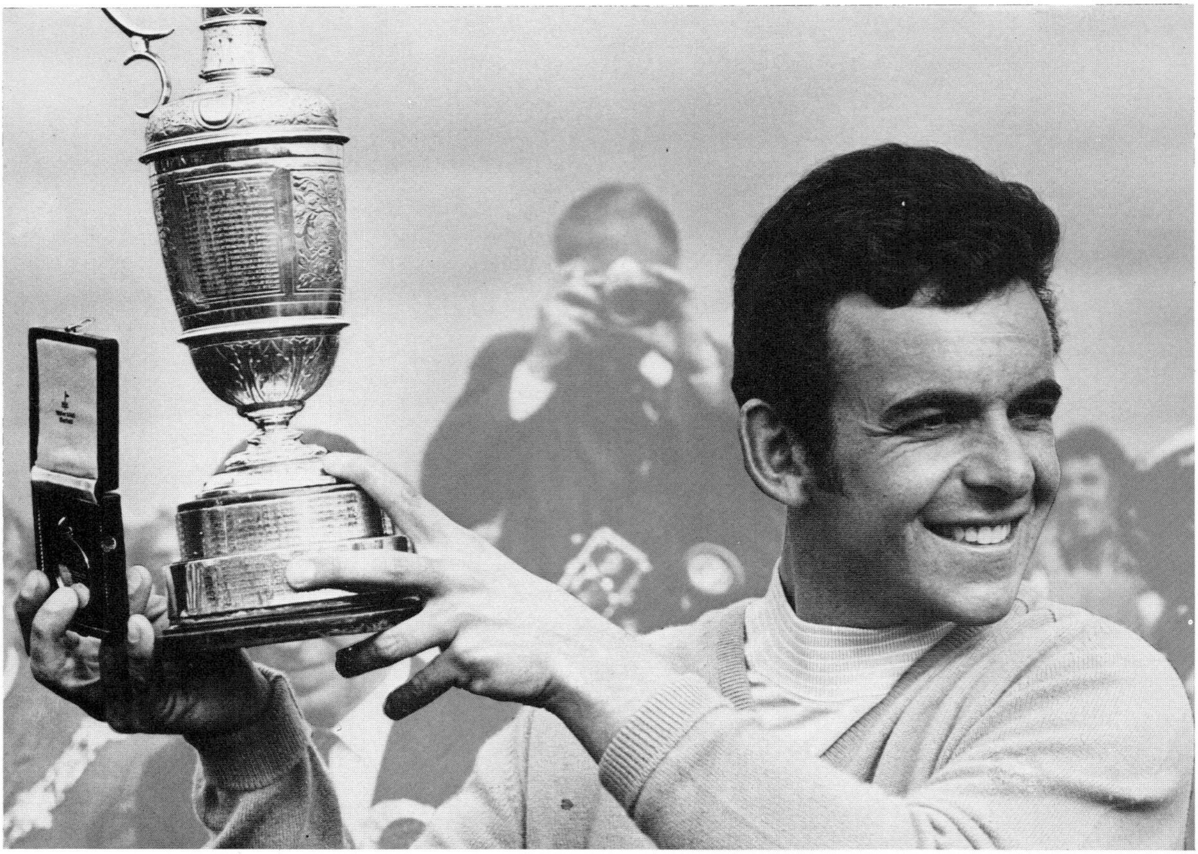

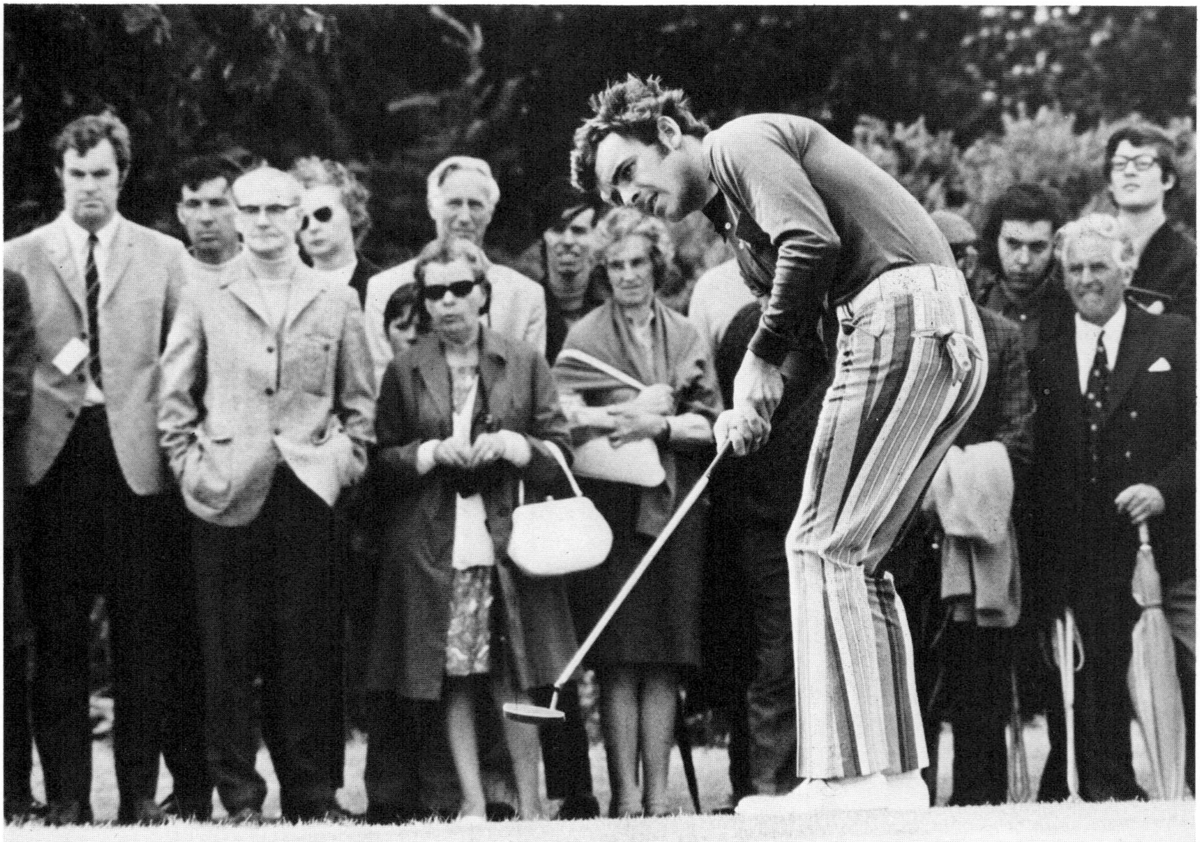

Tony Jacklin

"I count myself incredibly lucky to have won both the British and U.S. titles so early in my career. Don't forget that you can be a really great golfer and never win an Open Championship."

"I used to say to myself that whatever happened nothing could change me and the way I feel about life. Although I get really tense when going for the big ones, I never thought that the pressures would build up the way they have."

"I play golf because I love the game. What Lee Trevino did to me in the last two rounds of the 1972 Open took a terrible lot out of me. Had I not been conditioned by playing regularly in the top class it would have taken more."

157

"When you get anxious over a birdie-putt you very often fail to take the putter blade the whole way back — you want to get the stroke over with, put the ball in the hole and mark a two on your card."

"The crowds at home get excited about twice a year. The rest of the time they go along determined not to be thrilled or entertained. I have often had the impression that they clap only to keep their hands warm. All I can say is that the crowds in America get the adrenalin going and I sort of respond to their enthusiasm."

"I expect people will criticise me for playing the squire bit. But I don't think of all this in that way. The place is going to be a marvellous home in which to live and bring up the family. I can be happy anywhere but if I can be happy in a big house then maybe I am a little happier still. What the devil is wrong with that?"

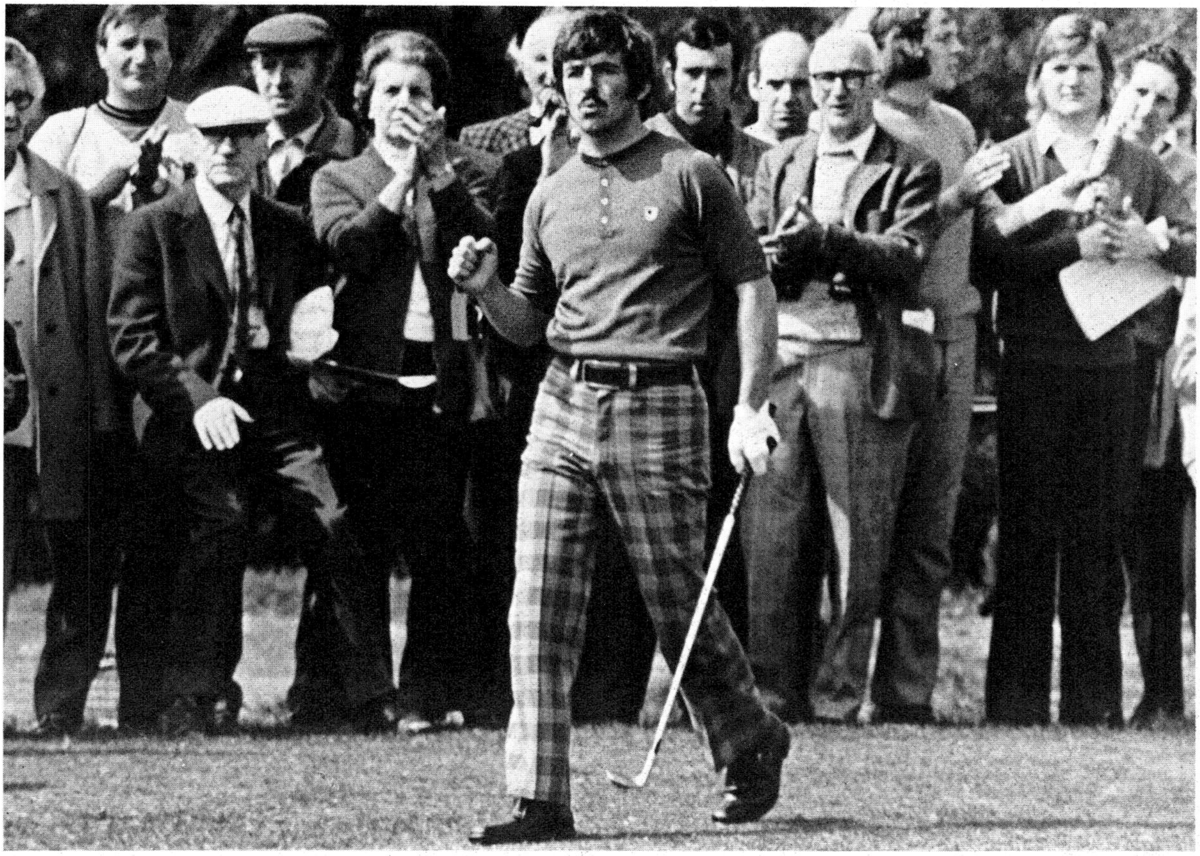

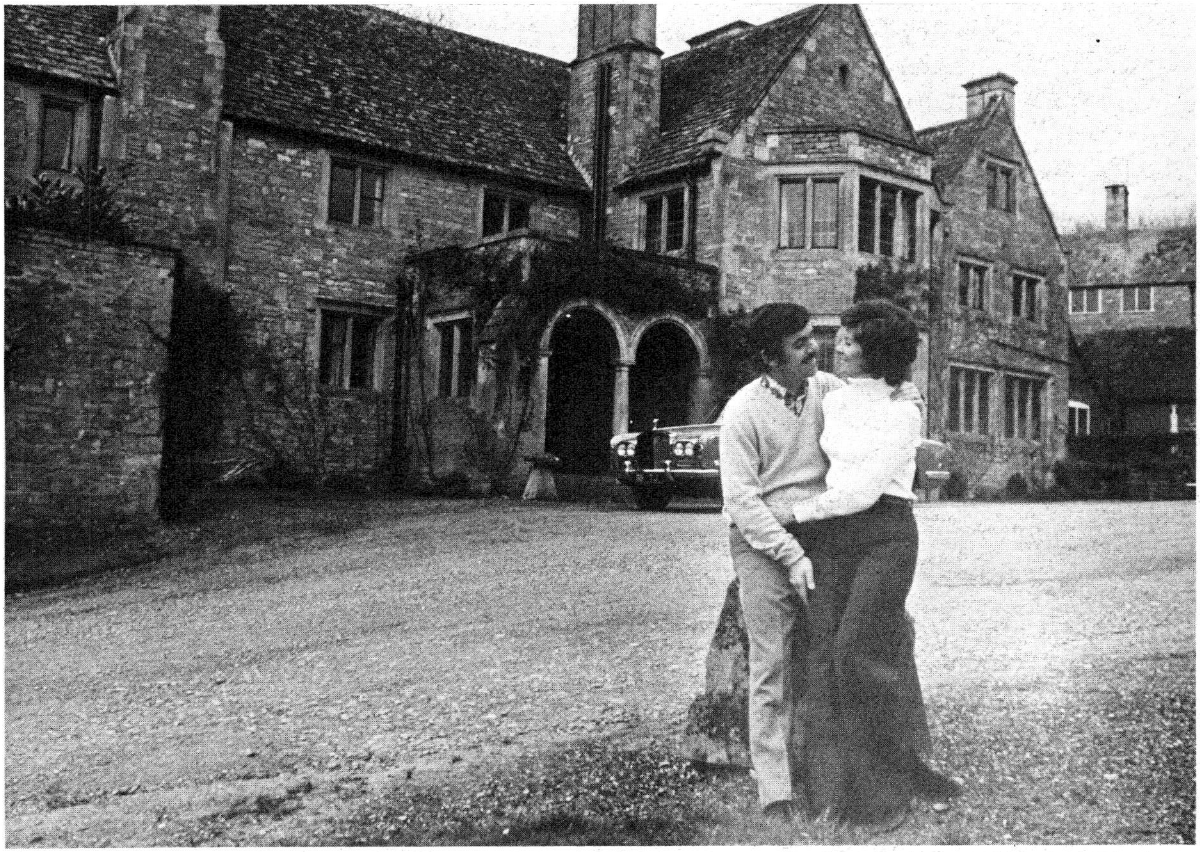

23
Ten of the World's Top Players

Bob Charles
Neil Coles
Bruce Crampton
Dave Hill
Tony Jacklin
Jack Nicklaus
Peter Oosterhuis
Juan Rodriguez
Lee Trevino
Tom Weiskopf

Plus a Portrait Gallery of
Leading International Tournament Stars

BOB CHARLES

Described as the greatest left-hander of all time, New Zealand's top golfer, Bob Charles, has many famous victories tucked under his belt. Not least of these were the 1963 Open Championship and the 1969 Piccadilly World Match-play Championship.

In 1972 Charles was having a lean time in America, playing steadily but seldom looking like a winner. Then, towards the end of the season he came to Britain and promptly picked up the Player Classic and Dunlop Masters titles – £17,000 for two weeks work is good by any standards.

Through the winter he played on the South African circuit with success, the highlight being victory in the South African Open.

Rumour has it he plans to play more golf in Britain. If that is the case, the British tour can only be enhanced by his presence.

NEIL COLES

The quiet man of the British circuit, Neil Coles is the player his fellow-professionals have voted the most consistent on the British and European tour. His career began in 1950, the year he took up the game and turned professional and he has won 22 major tournaments since his first in 1961.

Among the top 10 in the Order of Merit since 1962, he did not have, by his standards, one of his most successful years in 1972. He only won once – in the Scottish Open – and was in the top 10 just six other times!

His 1973 start was fantastic. In no time at all he had won three events – the Spanish Open, the Sumrie Better-Ball (with Bernard Hunt) and the Benson and Hedges Matchplay. On top of all these individual crowns, he has represented Britain and Ireland in the Ryder Cup six times, and played for England in the World Cup.

Not a bad record for a man whom many believe could succeed in America if he was prepared to travel – a pastime he refuses to do by air.

162

BRUCE CRAMPTON

This unsung Australian who won his first event on the American tour back in 1961, has built himself a reputation for stamina and dedication and a rapidly increasing bank balance.

Since 1969 he has always earned around £50,000 a season on the circuit and in 1972 he managed it without adding to his 10 previous tour wins. However, the fact that only Jack Nicklaus finished ahead of him in both the U.S. Open and the U.S. Masters and that he was third twice and fourth twice, helped him end 14th in the money-winners' list.

It should also have served as a warning to his fellow-professionals that Crampton was about to launch a devastating attack on the 1973 circuit which would see him with four wins under his belt and over £80,000 in his pocket by the end of June.

It meant he was earning more money from the tour than anyone – including Nicklaus – and it meant world acclaim for a man who should have been recognised long ago.

163

DAVE HILL

World golf is full of colourful players, not the least being outspoken American Dave Hill, whose volatile temperament has had him in trouble with the authorities more than once. This image has tended to cloud the fact that Hill is one of the most consistent players on the U.S. circuit.

His first year on tour was a struggle but since then he has never been out of the top 60. The high spot was 1969, when he finished second with the best stroke average on tour.

A player who finds the nervous strain so great that he loses anything up to 30 lb during a tournament season, Hill confesses his real ambition is to develop the perfect swing. But he also vows: "I will only play golf as long as it is fun." Early in 1973 he won the Memphis title for the fourth time holding off strong challenges from Lee Trevino and Johnny Miller. This victory and the fact that his swing seemed to be at its best must have been a pleasant present on his 36th birthday.

TONY JACKLIN

The man who brought British golf to life when he won the Open Championships of Britain and America in 1969 and 1970, the first British holder of the U.S. crown since Ted Ray some 50 years before, Jacklin is the number one crowd-puller in home events and just as popular during his American appearances.

A rare golfer, he has proved himself in many a tense situation, being able to concentrate and produce the right shot at the most critical moment. He appears to thrive on tension.

No doubt his early decision to tackle the U.S. circuits has had much to do with his attitude to the game. His most recent plans mean he is making assaults on the home tour, closely chased by leading rival Peter Oosterhuis.

Jacklin had a fine 1972 season with one American win and seven P.G.A. tour finishes in the top five. But his efforts to make the Open title his for the second time were thwarted by Lee Trevino. It was Trevino again who frustrated Jacklin's efforts in the Piccadilly World Match-play. The British star went round Wentworth in the second round of their match in around 63 shots – one his best-ever displays. But Trevino still hung on to win at the 36th.

For his contribution to British golf Jacklin was honoured by the Queen with an O.B.E. and the P.G.A. created him a life vice-president.

JACK NICKLAUS

With so little space it is difficult to know what facts about Jack Nicklaus to put in and what to leave out. On an overall basis it is fact that this world-beater has won well over £500,000 on the U.S. tour alone since turning professional in 1961.

It is also fact that 44 major titles have come his way plus two successes in the British Open and victory over Lee Trevino in the final of the Piccadilly World Matchplay.

Nicklaus has made such a success of playing the game that he has now branched out with various successful business ventures.

Last season was average by the great man's standards. He won seven events and was second three times. Major feature of the year was centred on his visit to Britain for the Open. He was already U.S. Masters and Open champion and the British Open was the third leg in his bid for the grand slam.

It is history how Lee Trevino won the event with Nicklaus only letting himself play attacking golf on the final day and just failing to win.

As 1973 got under way Nicklaus was soon back in the groove, winning four titles in the early part of the year to bring his tally to 48.

166

PETER OOSTERHUIS

Peter Oosterhuis, the man most likely to be making news for the next decade, is already picking up golf titles galore after five years as a professional.

A short, but brilliant, amateur record brought him international honours when at 19 he was a Walker Cup player, later being placed third in individual aggregates during the Eisenhower Trophy.

His first P.G.A. season saw him 17th in the Order of Merit, in 1970 he was seventh, and top in 1971 and 1972.

In his Ryder Cup début he scored singles victories over Arnold Palmer and Gene Littler. In 1970 his winnings were over the £10,000 mark, and again in 1971.

Last year he won £18,525 on the P.G.A. circuit alone. Through the winter and early 1973 he won the Maracaibo and French Opens, the South African Match-play and the Piccadilly Medal and was in the top 10 at least eight other times.

But his greatest showing to date, captivating the imagination of countless British televiewers was his third place in the 1973 U.S. Masters. Leading comfortably after three rounds, he let Tommy Aaron and J. C. Snead slip past.

JUAN RODRIGUEZ

For years this man has been known as the comic of the U.S. tour – not because he lacks golfing skill but because he excels at making spectators laugh. But recently this talented Puerto Rican whom everybody calls Chi Chi has changed his attitude and the benefits seem to be showing.

Prior to the 1972 season he had won five tour events in 10 years. Last year the fit, newly dedicated man won the Byron Nelson Classic after a play-off with Billy Casper, was second in the Philadelphia Classic and third twice. It helped push him up the money-winners' list from 74th to 12th.

If this fresh success proves attractive enough to Rodriguez, his wise-cracking days are over and this 38-year-old's early 1973 form certainly looks to be following the new pattern.

The man who runs to keep fit and claims to live on steak won the Greater Greensboro, was third in Florida and fourth in the Tournament of Champions.

Chi Chi must find winning amusing enough. Some of his opponents must be regretting the day he decided to change his outlook.

LEE TREVINO

The man who brings fun into the game and whether playing good or poor golf invariably seems to hit the headlines.

He really came into the world scene when taking the U.S. Open in 1968 and has been rolling in the cash ever since. On the U.S. tour alone the last five years have produced 13 titles and something like £300,000 in the bank, while in Britain he was runner-up to Jack Nicklaus in the 1970 Piccadilly Match-play Championship and to Tom Weiskopf last year, and winner of the British Open Championship in 1971 and 1972.

With that record he can afford to be funny . . . and the crowd love it.

He did not come on to the tour until he had completed seven years, hard years, as a professional, and if it had not been for his wife, who sent in his first U.S. Open entrance form, Trevino may well have been way out in the wilderness for a few more years. However, that entrance form led him to fifth place in his first Open and on to the road that has brought a much needed air of freshness to many a tournament.

He still lives in El Paso, where he started, with his family of three.

169

TOM WEISKOPF

Jack Nicklaus has said of Tom Weiskopf: "I hope he never discovers how good he really is. If he does we will all be in trouble!"

That is an opinion which has to be respected and Weiskopf is beginning to take heed of the compliment. For several years he has been a leading American money-winner, but it is only recently he has been showing the world what he really can achieve.

In 1968, for instance, he finished third in the U.S. money-winners' list after his first two tour wins. In 1971 he finished 12th with two more wins and last year he moved up to sixth with a win and two seconds.

But perhaps his greatest successes to date were consecutive wins in the British and Canadian Open Championships of 1973. Another victory which endeared him to British fans was his victory in the Piccadilly World Match-Play in 1972.

Weiskopf's achievements are all the more amazing, for he refuses to devote too much time to practice. He maintains he must give his family enough time for a normal family life. A surprise philosophy for one of the smoothest swingers in the world game.

170

TOMMY AARON (U.S.)

Always the bridesmaid, never the bride, was how they tagged him . . . until the 1973 U.S. Masters that is. A professional since 1960, he was runner-up almost to the point of obsession, before he broke through to take the 1969 Canadian Open. A year later he carried off the Atlantic Classic. But 1971 and 1972 appeared no different. In 1971 he was third three times and was consistent enough to finish 30th overall. Last year he failed to win an event again, but was second four times – including the U.S.P.G.A. – and finished ninth overall with more than £45,000. Early 1973 seemed to be going the same way before he showed remarkable cool in winning the Masters by a shot from J. C. Snead. *Born February 22, 1937. Height 6 ft. 1 in. Weight 180 lb.*

BRIAN ALLIN (U.S.)

He got off to a great start on the American professional circuit by winning the 1971 Greater Greensboro after just 13 weeks on tour. This win, achieved with a 20-foot birdie putt at the first extra hole in a three-way play-off, was a courageous affair. He then faded out of the top 10, his next best being joint 17th. In 1972 he finished 56th in the money-winners' list, but early 1973 showed a remarkable change in fortunes, thanks to his second tour win in the Florida Citrus Open. It pushed him in 14th place among money-winners after three months of the season. *Born October 13, 1944. Height 5 ft. 9 in. Weight 135 lb.*

GEORGE ARCHER (U.S.)

Tallest player on the U.S. tour, had first win in the Lucky International, San Francisco. Since has won 10 tour events, including the 1969 Masters. One of the steadiest scorers on tour, he finished fourth in the 1971 money-winners'. Last year he moved up to third behind Nicklaus and Trevino, winning the Los Angeles Open and the Greater Greensboro Open and finishing second in the Tucson Open. Equal second in Tucson, 1973. *Born October 1, 1939. Height 6 ft. 6 in. Weight 200 lb.*

HUGH BAIOCCHI (S. Africa)

He won the South African amateur title in 1970, but did not go professional until November 1971. He was an instant success, finishing the South African season in third place overall. On the P.G.A. circuit he was in the top 10 on four occasions and finished 18th in the Order of Merit table with earnings of almost £3,000. Back in South Africa he had a double success, taking the Western Province title and the South African International Classic Championship and coming second in his country's P.G.A. Championship. Since then he has come joint fifth in the Italian Open and joint fourth in Madrid.
Born August 17, 1946. Height 6 ft. Weight 12 st. 7 lb.

HARRY BANNERMAN (U.K.)

An inspired three-month period in 1971, when he finished well in the money in 11 tournaments without recording a single win, gained Bannerman a place in the Ryder Cup team which faced America at St. Louis. He was unbeaten in singles encounters in the match. Winner of 10 Scottish events, including the Scottish P.G.A. in 1967. In that same year he represented Scotland in the World Cup in Mexico with Eric Brown. Last year he slipped to 16th in the Order of Merit, his best finish being second in the Benson and Hedges Festival.
Born March 5, 1942. Height 5 ft. 11 in. Weight 12 st. 3 lb.

MILLER BARBER (U.S.)

With less than £4,500 to show for his first four years on tour, Barber took a back seat to reconsider things. He came back 10 years ago and since has been really making news. In the past six years his total winnings have passed £170,000. He has seven tour winnings to his credit, the most recent being the Tucson Open last year. A member of the 1969 and 1971 U.S. Ryder Cup teams, he only missed his eighth tour win after two extra holes of a play-off with Jack Nicklaus in the 1973 Greater New Orleans Open.
Born March 31, 1931. Height 5 ft. 11 in. Weight 200 lb.

172

BRIAN BARNES (U.K.)

Consistency the keynote of success. He played in the last two Ryder Cup matches. Barnes finished fourth in the 1971 P.G.A. Order of Merit. First P.G.A. victory in 1969, taking the Agfa-color tournament and followed this by becoming Coca-Cola Champion. A year later he became the first British winner of the Wills Masters in Australia. Runner-up Italian Open in 1971. Last year he finished eighth in the Order of Merit with a win in the Martini and four other placings in the top 10. He was fifth in the 1973 Spanish Open.
Born June 3, 1945. Height 6 ft. 2 in. Weight 15 st. 5 lb.

FRANK BEARD (U.S.)

Since 1963 he has won 11 tournaments and been leading money-winner twice, yet few people really know him. Having won the Kentucky Amateur twice before turning professional, he brought to the pro tour an elegant swing and remarkable putting ability in 1962. In 1971 he won the New Orleans and tied for second place in the Byron Nelson Classic to finish eighth in the U.S. Tour money-winners' list. In 1972 he dropped to 40th, his best result being runner-up to Jack Nicklaus in the U.S. Pro Match-play. Finished second to Homero Blancas in 1973 Monsanto Open.
Born May 1, 1939. Height 6 ft. Weight 190 lb.

DEANE BEMAN (U.S.)

Following a fabulous amateur career, which included 1960 and 1963 U.S. Amateur Championships, the 1959 British Championship, membership of five U.S. Walker Cup teams and four U.S. World Amateur teams, Beman went professional in 1967. Since then he has won more than £100,000, including four tour victories. He won the Quad-Cities title in 1971 and ended the season 22nd in the money-winners' list. In 1972 he retained the Quad-Cities title and finished runner-up to Lee Trevino in the St. Louis Classic. It helped him to 21st place in the money-winners' list.
Born April 22, 1938. Height 5 ft. 7½ in. Weight 155 lb.

173

MAURICE BEMBRIDGE (U.K.)

A great traveller, playing in over 40 major stroke-play tournaments throughout the world in 1971. He won the Dunlop Masters and finished third in the P.G.A. Order of Merit. Won the Kenya Open (1968–69). Played in the Piccadilly World Match-play Championship 1969. Last year he won the Lusaka Open and ended 19th in the Order of Merit table. He then went travelling again. He was third in the Australia Open; second in the New Zealand Open and Zambia's Cock o' the North event and third in the Portuguese Open.
Born February 21, 1945. Height 5 ft. 7½ in. Weight 11 st. 6 lb.

HOMERO BLANCAS (U.S.)

In 1962, three years before turning professional, Blancas played his way into the record books by returning a 55 on the Premier Golf Course in Texas. It equalled the all-time low-scoring record. In his first year as a pro in 1965 he became Rookie-of-the-Year and since then has won four major titles. In 1971 his highspot was a round of 63 during the Phoenix Open but he improved in 1972, moving from 38th to 20th in the money-winners' list and winning the Phoenix Open. In the early part of 1973 he won the Monsanto Open and finished joint third in the Florida Citrus Open.
Born March 7, 1938. Height 5 ft. 10 in. Weight 195 lb.

GAY BREWER (U.S.)

A well-travelled professional since 1956, he has 10 major wins on his card plus the 1965 National Four-ball title. Beaten in a play-off for the Masters in 1966, he made sure the following year with a clear-cut margin. In 1972 he made a remarkable recovery. An internal haemorrhage at the U.S. Masters nearly killed him, but three months later he won the Canadian Open. This was the start of a cash bonanza which included second in the Player Classic and victory in the Pacific Masters. The three events netted £49,350. In early 1973 he was second in the Tucson Open.
Born March 12, 1932. Height 6 ft. Weight 173 lb.

ANDREW BROOKS (U.K.)

Unbeaten in three matches in the 1969 Walker Cup series in Milwaukee, he joined the professional ranks soon after and attained 26th placing in the 1970 P.G.A. Order of Merit in his first year. In 1971 represented Scotland in the Double Diamond International tournament. Last year his best showing was joint ninth in the Piccadilly Medal although consistent tournament play put him into 29th place in the Order of Merit.

Born December 22, 1946. Height 6 ft. 1 in. Weight 12 st. 7 lb.

STUART BROWN (U.K.)

A professional since 1965, he first attacked the circuit in 1970 and has since impressed the experts with steady consistency of performance. Won the Lusaka Dunlop Open in 1971 and same year tied for second place in the Penfold-Bournemouth tournament. Finishing 36th in the P.G.A. Order of Merit in his first year, he rose to 17th position in 1971. Last year was not such a success as he slipped to 56th and total prize money of £1,217.

Born August 11, 1946. Height 5 ft. 10½ in. Weight 12 st. 7 lb.

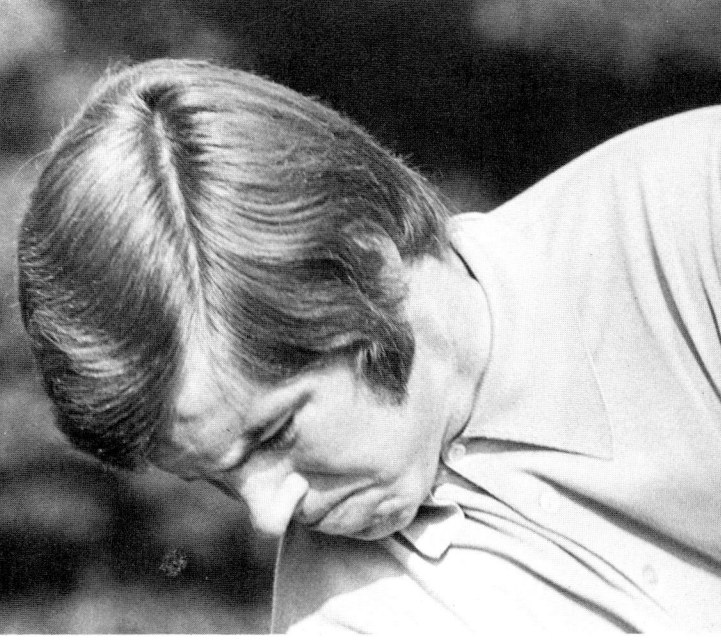

PETER BUTLER (U.K.)

In 14 years has won 15 major P.G.A. and overseas championships and been placed in the top 15 of the P.G.A. Order of Merit for the last 11 years. Represented Britain three times in Ryder Cup matches (1965, 1969 and 1971); he was also selected for England's winning team in the Double Diamond Home International in 1971. Won the Classic International at Copt Heath in 1971, was runner-up in the Benson and Hedges Golf Festival at Fulford, fifth in the Agfa-Gevaert tournament at Stoke Poges, third in the Martini International at Royal Norwich, fifth in Carrolls International, and finished seventh in the P.G.A. Order of Merit. He retained this position last year thanks to six tour finishes in the top 10. Early in 1973 he was fourth in the Spanish Open.

Born March 25, 1932. Height 6 ft. Weight 13 st.

175

BILLY CASPER (U.S.)

After 19 years as a professional and with winnings of over £500,000 in America alone, where he has won 50 major events, Casper has found it harder to stay in front in the last two years. In 1971 he had only one win and fell from second to 10th in the money-winners' list. In 1972 he failed to manage even that, his best finish being second in the Byron Nelson Classic, and he slipped to 40th in the list. But his ability is undisputed for he has won the U.S. Open twice and the Masters once. He finished second in the San Diego early in 1973.

Born June 24, 1931. Height 5 ft. 11 in. Weight 185 lb.

CLIVE CLARK (U.K.)

Following a brilliant amateur career, he turned professional in 1965 and registered his first major success the following year when taking the Danish Open. Tied for third place with Gary Player in the Open Championship, 1967 and that year finished third in the P.G.A. Order of Merit. Following a short American trip he returned to take the Agfacolor tournament, and later the Bowmaker tournament in 1968. He won the John Player Trophy in 1970, but has failed to take another tour title since then. In 1972 he was second in the French Open and had four other top 10 placings. Early in 1973 he was third in the Madrid Open.

JIM COLBERT (U.S.)

In seven years on the U.S. tour Colbert has managed just two wins. The first was at Monsanto in 1969 and the second last year in the Greater Milwaukee Open. In fact 1972 was a very good year for him, for he was also second once and third once as he raced up the money-winners' list from 59th to 23rd. And 1973 began well, for he won the Greater Jacksonville and finished third in the Tournament of Champions.

Born March 9, 1941. Height 5 ft. 9 in. Weight 165 lb.

176

Five times running Ronnie Shade was winner of the Scottish Amateur Championship, three times victor in the Brabazon Trophy and played four times for Britain in the Walker Cup team. Just at the time when it seemed that he had left it too late to turn professional, he joined the paid ranks in 1968 and immediately celebrated by winning the major Carrolls tournament in Dublin.

Two of Hunt's rivals this season have been young Scots pro Bernard Gallacher (left) and South African Hugh Baiocchi, now representing Scottish golf club Ely on the British circuit.

Guy Hunt, 11 inches shorter than his giant opponent Peter Oosterhuis, nevertheless finished a close second to the Dulwich pro in last year's Order of Merit table. Hunt won a total of almost £10,000.

At the age of 23 Bob Dickson won both the
British and American Amateur Championships
in the same year. Since turning professional he has
moved steadily up the American money-winners'
table, holding a regular place among the leaders
throughout the season.

Old campaigner Billy Casper (left) and newcomer Jerry
Heard. While Casper has amassed more than 1,500,000
dollars in a 20-year pro career, Heard has collected in excess of
200,000 dollars in less than four full seasons on tour.

Stockily built Jim Jamieson, born in Kalamazoo, qualified for the full U.S. tour in the autumn of 1968 and continues to make steady progress up the money-winners' charts.

Dave Hill has been an outspoken member of the American circuit since 1959 – yet he is quite capable of letting his golf do the talking. In a constant search for perfection he was the lowest scorer throughout 1969 with a stroke average of 70·344.

Maurice Bembridge is one of Britain's most-travelled professional competitors, having played in nearly 50 major stroke-play tournaments across the world. He played in the Piccadilly World Match-Play in 1969.

CHARLES COODY (U.S.)

Winner of 30 titles before turning professional in 1964 he has been a high-ranking money-winner ever since. Although only winning three major titles, including the Masters in 1971, he has been there or thereabouts on numerous occasions. But a little inconsistency has cost him dear. In 1971 he finished 16th in the money-winners' list but 1972 was not so successful. Highest places were two thirds and he dropped to 37th in the money-winners' list. He was second in the 1973 Florida Citrus Open.
Born July 13, 1937. Height 6 ft. 2 in. Weight 185 lb.

GORDON CUNNINGHAM (U.K.)

A professional for 17 years, his early seasons were mainly spent overseas, but in his second year on the P.G.A. tour he took third place in the Penfold tournament. That was in 1968 and he later won the Cutty Sark tournament and the Glasgow Professional Championship. Scottish P.G.A. Champion in 1969, he also won the Uniroyal tournament that year. Last year he improved 14 places on 1971, to finish 31st in the Order of Merit, even though his best performance was joint 14th in the Player Trophy and the Sumrie Better-Ball.
Born June 1, 1934. Height 5 ft. 8 in. Weight 11 st.

KIM DABSON (U.K.)

Turned professional in 1969. Met with mixed fortune in early British events. Pipped at the post by Peter Butler in the 1971 Classic International, he had earlier finished fifth in the Martini, and was well placed in the Gallaher Ulster Open and the Benson and Hedges Festival. This earned him 37th place in the P.G.A. Order of Merit, comparing well with his 63rd position of the previous year. Last year he was joint 11th in two events, but could not maintain consistency and slid 10 places down the table.
Born July 10, 1952. Height 6 ft. Weight 11 st. 7 lb.

185

CRAIG DEFOY (U.K.)

One of the few professionals to join the ranks straight from school at the age of 16. It was eight years before he hit world headlines when finishing a sound fourth in the 1971 Open Championship, three strokes behind Lee Trevino. In 1968 he won the Gor-Ray Under-24. In 1971 he finished third in the W. D. and H. O. Wills Open, fourth in the Martini, and reached the semi-finals of the Piccadilly Medal. In 1972 he won the Zambian and Mufuliva Opens and retained the Zambian title this year. He finished second in the 1973 Spanish Open.

Born March 27, 1947. Height 6 ft. 1 in. Weight 11 st. 5 lb.

BRUCE DEVLIN (Australia)

A professional for 11 years and a much travelled golfer, his U.S. tour record shows nine major successes including three, the Bob Hope Classic, Cleveland Open and Alcan in 1970. That year he finished 11th in the money-winners' list. Best performance in 1971 was to tie runner-up spot in the Tournament of Champions, and finish second in the National Team event. Last year was a more successful one as he moved to ninth in the money-winners' list, thanks to two wins and a second. He then returned to Australia to share third place in the Masters.

Born October 10, 1937. Height 6 ft. 1 in. Weight 158 lb.

BOB DICKSON (U.S.)

He compiled an outstanding amateur record on both sides of the Atlantic, culminating in victory in both the British and American amateur championships in 1967. His best professional finish in 1971 was third in the Sahara and he failed to figure at all in 1972. But early 1973 saw the great breakthrough when he held off a chasing bunch of four to win the San Diego Open. This seemed to be the spur as he finished third in the Byron Nelson Classic and inside four months had settled in 10th place among the money-winners.

Born January 25, 1944. Height 6 ft. 3 in. Weight 190 lb.

JAN DORRESTEIN (Holland)

He turned professional in 1966 and soon became the most successful Dutch golfer of his time. He won his native title in 1970 and 1971 and is a constant Dutch choice for the World Cup. In 1970 he won the Kenyan title and he repeated this triumph this year. A steady P.G.A. tour in 1972 earned him 35th place in the Order of Merit.
Born September 8, 1945. Height 5 ft. 10 in. Weight 154 lb.

LEE ELDER (U.S.)

It took 39-year-old Lee Elder around nine years to break into the U.S. tour pro ranks, in spite of being regarded as one of the top coloured golfers in America. He has yet to win a tour event, but came near to success in 1971 when finishing tied second for the Thomas Memphis behind Lee Trevino, and tied third for the New Orleans Open. Perhaps his best performance was in 1968 when tied first place with Jack Nicklaus for the American Golf Classic and took him to five holes in the play-off before yielding. In 1972 he finished second twice and was 32nd in the money-winners' list. Early in 1973 he was in contention several times but the first win and a place in the Masters eluded him.
Born July 14, 1934. Height 5 ft. 8 in. Weight 170 lb.

RAY FLOYD (U.S.)

His greatest year was 1969, six years after he joined the U.S. tour. He had three wins, which began with the Jacksonville, continued with the American Golf Classic and culminated in the U.S.P.G.A. That year he earned over £40,000 and finished eighth in the money-winners' list. Since then he has slipped rapidly down the scale. In 1972 he finished 70th. Early this year he began to show sparks of his old form and only lost the Crosby title after a play-off with Nicklaus.
Born September 4, 1942. Height 6 ft. Weight 185 lb.

187

ROD FUNSETH (U.S.)

A professional golfer since 1956, but not a U.S. tourer until 1962, Funseth has had only one outright victory – the 1965 Phoenix Open. 1971 was his best year since then, when he was second once and third twice to finish 34th in the money-winners' list. He got off to a great start in 1973 when he won in Los Angeles and joined the top 10 money-winners.
Born April 3, 1933. Height 5 ft. 10 in. Weight 170 lb.

BERNARD GALLACHER (U.K.)

An enthusiastic golfer since early schooldays, at 17 he won the Scottish Stroke-play Championship and represented his country one year later. Turned professional the same year. In 1969 he won four tournaments and took the Harry Vardon Trophy as well as representing Britain in the Ryder Cup. He had taken the W. D. and H. O. Wills Open at Moor Park having broken the course record with 63. In 1970 he had one victory and slid to 22nd in the Order of Merit, but he was back in 1971. He took the Martini and played in his second Ryder Cup match. Last year he finished 12th in the Order of Merit. Early in 1973 he lost the Portuguese title after a play-off.
Born February 9, 1949. Height 5 ft. 9 in. Weight 11 st. 5 lb.

ANGEL GALLARDO (Spain)

Following his first major success in the Portuguese Open in 1967, he has been a popular and successful figure in American, British and European events. In 1969, with Maurice Bembridge as partner, he shared the Sumrie Four-ball tournament. He won the Spanish Open in 1970 and last year was the only European to win on the American continent when taking the Mexican Open. Represented Spain in the World Cup in 1970 and 1971 and took the Marlboro Nations Cup with Valentin Barrios last year. In 1972 he also had three finishes in the top 10 on the P.G.A. circuit and early in 1973 he finished fourth in the Maracaibo and Caracas Opens.
Height 5 ft. 7 in. Weight 11st. 7 lb.

JEAN GARAIALDE (France)

A leading European golfer for the last 11 years, he has been French Champion on nine occasions. Won Open Championships of Spain, France and Germany in 1969. In 1970, apart from again winning the German Open, beat Jack Nicklaus by two strokes to take the Volvo tournament in Sweden. This year he finished third in the Italian Open. *Born October 2, 1934. Height 5 ft. 10 in. Weight 12 st.*

JOHN GARNER (U.K.)

A three-handicap player when 16, he joined the professional ranks that year and has steadily improved. In 1967 he was second in the Under-23 Championship, 1969 saw him second in the Algarve Open, second in the Schweppes P.G.A. Championship as well as the Martini International. He ended that year 13th in the P.G.A. Order of Merit. An injury marred his 1970 programme which included second place in the Nigerian Open. In 1971 he won the Coca-Cola Championship and finished well up in 10 tournaments to earn 12th spot in the P.G.A. Order of Merit and a place in the Ryder Cup team at St. Louis. Last year he scored his first major victory in the Benson and Hedges Match-play and with four other top 10 placings moved to sixth in the Order of Merit. Early in 1973 he was joint fourth in the Portuguese Open. *Born January 9, 1947. Height 5 ft. 10 in. Weight 10 st. 12 lb.*

BOB GOALBY (U.S.)

Won six amateur tournaments in the two years before turning professional in 1957, since when he has been a regular tour player. Most important win was the 1968 Masters, the year Roberto de Vicenzo signed for an incorrect score, but other wins have included Greensboro, Coral Gables, Los Angeles, St. Petersburg, San Diego, Heritage Classic and in 1971, the Bahamas National. His position in the money-winners' list has fluctuated from year to year but is rarely out of the first 60. *Born March 14, 1931. Height 6 ft. Weight 195 lb.*

DAVID GRAHAM (Australia)

He has made remarkable progress since starting out on the American circuit. In 1971 he finished 135th on tour, but last year he raced up to 35th after winning the Cleveland Open and finished second in Houston. He then returned to Australia where he was runner-up in both the Dunlop International and the Open. In the latter he only failed after a play-off. He also lost after four holes of a play-off in the Pacific Masters.

Born May 23, 1946. Height 5 ft. 9½ in. Weight 10 st. 9 lb.

LOU GRAHAM (U.S.)

Since joining the U.S. tour in 1964, Graham has shown gradual improvement in the money-winners' list. In 1971 he reached 23rd place after a very busy season. He competed 35 events, finished 29 and was in the top 10 ten times, but he failed to win an event that year to add to his 1967 victory in Minnesota. Last year he doubled his winning total with victory in the Liggett and Myers Open and that, coupled with a second and a third, pushed him up to 19th place. He made a great start to 1973 with two equal seconds and a third in the first four months.

Born January 7, 1938. Height 6 ft. Weight 175 lb.

HUBERT GREEN (U.S.)

Hubert Green, after a quiet beginning to the pro circuit, stormed into the limelight in 1971 with a play-off victory in the Houston event, a second and a third as well as several other high placings. In 1972 he went off the boil a little, slipping from 29th to 58th in the money-winners' list. But early 1973 saw a return to form with his second tour victory in the Tallahassee Open.

Born December 28, 1946. Height 6 ft. 1 in. Weight 170 lb.

190

MALCOLM GREGSON (U.K.)

At 16 he reached the final of the French Boys' Championship and represented England and Britain in boys' teams. Turning professional in 1961 he waited three years before his first real success, taking the Gor-Ray Assistants' Championship. Gained worldwide experience during 1965–66, visiting America, the Far East, Australasia and South Africa. In 1970 he finished 17th in the P.G.A. Order of Merit, but went back to 24th placing in 1971 despite a sound performance in the Open Championship. He won the 1972 Sumrie with Brian Huggett and was joint second in the Dutch Open. In early 1973 he finished second in the Nigerian Open.

Born August 15, 1943. Height 6 ft. Weight 12 st.

DALE HAYES (South Africa)

A scratch player at 15, he proved an outstanding amateur at international level. Twice winner of the South African Stroke-play Championship, he also won the German Amateur Championship. Joined the professional ranks in 1971 and took the Spanish Open Championship that year. Earlier he had won the Newcastle Open in South Africa, and since has taken the Bert Hagerman tournament with a five-stroke margin. Last winter he had a tremendous South African season, winning twice, coming second twice, third once, fourth once and fifth once.

Born July 1, 1952. Height 6 ft. 3½ in. Weight 14 st.

JERRY HEARD (U.S.)

A tour player since 1969, he followed up high placings in the Cleveland and Philadelphia Opens with a fourth in the Westchester, which pushed him well up the cash list. A win in the American Golf Classic, tied second in the Danny Thomas-Memphis, tied third in the Western, tied fourth in the Crosby National, Citrus and Cleveland events plus high placings in both the National Airlines and Bahamas. Winner Florida Citrus Open and Colonial Invitation, 1972.

Born May 1, 1947. Height 6 ft. Weight 190 lb.

191

VINCE HOOD (U.K.)

Winner of the Gor-Ray Assistant Professional Championship in 1966, he has maintained a steady P.G.A. rating since. From 33rd placing in the Order of Merit (1967) he moved to 25th in 1968, and in 1971 following sound performances in the Penfold-Bournemouth and the Dunlop Masters he finished 23rd. Last year was even better as he climbed two more places to 21st, thanks to five finishes in the top 15. Highlight was joint second in the Player Trophy.

Born September 3, 1942. Height 5 ft. 11½ in. Weight 15 st.

TOMMY HORTON (U.K.)

Since his first major tournament success Horton has been a regular winner on all major circuits, but in 1970 he really hit the headlines. He became the first British winner of the South African Open Championship, and took the runner-up spot in both the Piccadilly Medal and Gallaher Ulster Opens. In 1971 he was 13th in the table and this time won the Gallaher Ulster Open. Last year he won the Piccadilly Medal and finished 15th in the Order of Merit. Early in 1973 he won the Nigerian Open, but his tour start was quiet.

Born June 16, 1941. Height 5 ft. 8½ in. Weight 9 st. 11 lb.

BRIAN HUGGETT (U.K.)

Brian Huggett is firmly established as a formidable tournament golfer He has represented Britain on four occasions in Ryder Cup matches, and Wales eight times in the World Cup. A professional since 1951, he has won every major honour in Britain except the Open Championship in which he was runner-up to Peter Thomson in 1965, and third in 1962. In 1971 Huggett represented Wales in the Double Diamond International and the World Cup. He partnered Malcolm Gregson to win the Sumrie better ball last year, but failed to win a major individual title for the first time in five years. Best show was second in the Italian Open.

Born November 18, 1936. Height 5 ft. 6 in. Weight 11 st. 10 lb.

WARREN HUMPHREYS (U.K.)

The teenage English amateur champion and 1971 Walker Cup hero made a fine professional start in South Africa and came 33rd in the British Order of Merit after a steady season in which joint 18th in the Masters was his best performance. The South African appears to be a lucky event for him, for he finished fifth in the 1973 event. He wasted outright success with a final round 76.
Born April 1, 1952. Height 5 ft. 10½ in. Weight 12 st.

BERNARD HUNT (U.K.)

Since 1946, he has played all over the world and has won events in seven overseas countries, including the championships of Brazil, Egypt, France, Belgium and Germany. His remarkable success started in 1953 with his first P.G.A. win in the Spalding tournament. In the top 12 of the Order of Merit list seven times in the past 13 years, he has represented Britain eight times in the Ryder Cup and played six times for England in the World Cup. Last year he was in the top 10 in three tour events and early in 1973 celebrated selection as Ryder Cup captain by winning the Sumrie event in partnership with Neil Coles.
Born February 2, 1930. Height 6 ft. 2½ in. Weight 14 st.

GUY HUNT (U.K.)

Steadily climbed the Order of Merit list in 1971 to finish 15th, following a placing of 30th the previous year. Won the Southern P.G.A. Championship 1968 and same year was successful in Lord Derby's Under-23 tournament. In 1971 he reached quarter-finals of the Piccadilly Medal and was runner-up in the Coca-Cola Championship. Last year was the best yet as he shot to second in the Order of Merit with 11 finishes in the top 10.
Born January 17, 1947. Height 5 ft. 6 in. Weight 10 st. 8 lb.

193

HALE IRWIN (U.S.)

Since joining the U.S. tour in 1968, Irwin has had hardly a lean patch. He has shown steady improvement in the money-winners' list from 117th in 1968 to 13th in 1971. It was in this year that he recorded his first tour victory in the Heritage Classic and finished second in two others. In 1972 he continued to succeed, with three second placings and three thirds.
Born June 3, 1945. Height 6 ft. Weight 170 lb.

HUGH JACKSON (U.K.)

Taking to the game when 16, he turned professional six years later. In 1968 teamed with Richard Emery to take the Piccadilly Four-ball tournament, and later that year won the Irish Dunlop. In 1970 finished eighth in Open Championship, third in Daks, fourth in Carrolls International. Won the Irish Professional Championship and finished ninth in the money-winners' list. In 1971 he represented Ireland in the Double Diamond Home International and took the Ulster Professional Championship for the sixth time. Last year he was in the top 10 in four P.G.A. tour events but never close to a win.
Born February 28, 1940. Height 5 ft. $8\frac{1}{2}$ in. Weight 10 st. 9 lb.

JIM JAMIESON (U.S.)

Consistently improving Jim Jamieson has become a man to reckon with on the U.S. tour since joining it in 1969. In 1971 his best finish was joint fifth and 63rd place in the money-winners' list. Last year he won the Western Open, was third in the Florida Citrus and caught the public eye with his joint second in the U.S.P.G.A. behind Gary Player. On that occasion he was tied with Tommy Aaron and it was Aaron he contended with again in the 1973 Masters. Aaron won, Jamieson was joint third.
Born April 21, 1943. Height 5 ft. 10 in. Weight 210 lb.

194

NICK JOB (U.K.)

In 1969 and 1970 he showed exceptional promise and was spoken of as a future tournament star. Most of the optimism had stemmed from the fact that he won the Gor-Ray Under-24 event in 1969 and the B.U.A. Rising Star even the following year. However, an injury put him out of tour action for a year and it says much for his courage that he fought back successfully enough last year to finish joint third in the German Open and equal seventh in the Swiss. His efforts pushed him up to 27th in the Order of Merit table. *Born July 27, 1949. Height 6 ft. 1 in. Weight 11 st. 7 lb.*

GRIER JONES (U.S.)

Grier Jones had one of the most meteoric rises up the U.S. money-winners' list on record in 1972 after three years on tour. He had been struggling a little to keep his head above water with a best place of joint sixth in 1971 and a money-winners' position of 72nd. Before 1972 was two months old he was Hawaiian champion and he continued to produce consistent winning golf, culminating in his second win in the Robinson Fall Classic. This helped him to finish the fourth richest tourer of the season. *Born May 6, 1946. Height 5 ft. 10 in. Weight 164 lb.*

JIMMY KINSELLA (U.K.)

A sound performer since schooldays (he won three Boys' Championships), he became professional at Castle when 26. Success in Carrolls International early in 1967 was his first big win, but three seasons later he gained 10th position in the P.G.A. Order of Merit, following a series of fine performances in the Alcan International, Long John Scotch Whisky Match-play Championship, and the Penfold. In 1971 he won Irish Dunlop and finished third in Irish Professional Championship. Represented Ireland 1968 and 1969. Last year he won the Madrid Open and became Irish pro champion, moving to 40th in the Order of Merit. He finished fourth in his 1973 defence in Madrid. *Born May 25, 1939. Height 6 ft. Weight 12 st. 7 lb.*

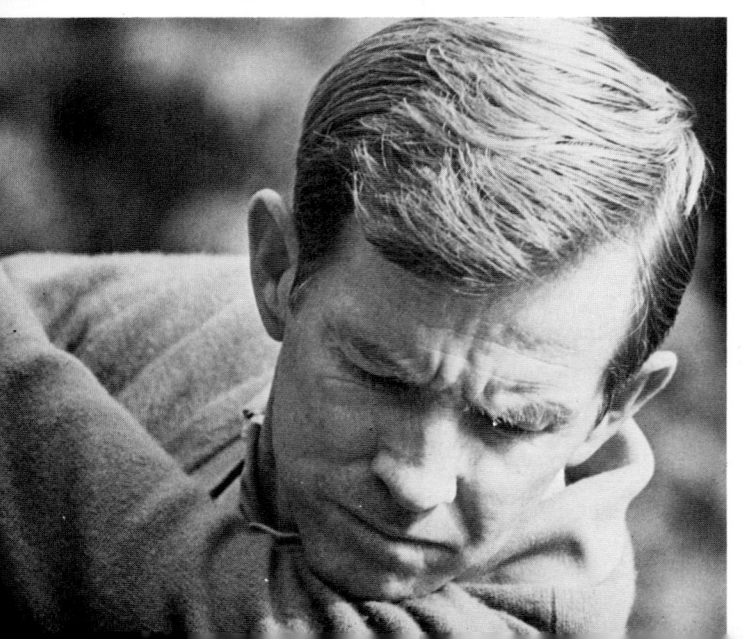

GEORGE KNUDSON (Canada)

Moves frequently between the U.S. and Canada where he was born and has been a regular tour player for 13 years. Has won almost £140,000 in that time, with 11 major wins on the card. In 1964, apart from the Canadian P.G.A. Championship, he picked up wins at Caracas and Fresno, but his highest placing came a year later when a New Orleans victory helped towards a 22nd position in the money list. Out of touch during 1971, when his highest placing was tied third in the Colonial, Knudson slipped to 60th position which just saved him from qualifying for the 1972 campaign. He halved this placing last year thanks to victory in the Kaiser International.

Born June 28, 1937. Height 5 ft. 10 in. Weight 165 lb.

GENE LITTLER (U.S.) *bottom left*

A quiet man, Littler has been a popular tour star since 1954, and in the 19 years since has won something like £350,000 with no fewer than 23 tournament successes. Winner of the U.S. Open in 1961, he won the Tournament of Champions three years in a row, 1955–56–57. A member of the Ryder Cup team six times, he won two more titles in 1971 before contracting cancer. It says much for his fighting qualities that he recovered to remain among the top 50 money-winners in the first half of 1973.

Born July 21, 1930. Height 5 ft. 9½ in. Weight 165 lb.

JOHN MAHAFFEY (U.S.)

Very few new boys on the U.S. tour can have bettered the gigantic leap up the money-winners' list made by John McLaffey. He graduated for the tour in 1971 and his best finish that year was a tie for 12th. Just 12 months, one second and one third later McLaffey had leaped from 230th to 39th in the list, increasing his wages from $2,010 to $50,886. He had only limited success early in 1973.

Born May 9, 1948. Height 5 ft. 9 in. Weight 140 lb.

196

DOUG McCLELLAND (U.K.)

Turning professional at 20 after representative honours in Youth Internationals, in 1971 he tied for fourth place in the Daks tournament and later did well in the Swiss Open and also the W. D. and H. O. Wills Open. During the South African tour in 1970–71 he performed well in several important events. He finished in 30th position in the P.G.A. Order of Merit for 1971. Last year he was second in two events, ninth in one and 10th in two and moved to 22nd in the Order of Merit. He came close to his first tour win in the Benson and Hedges Match-play, losing in the final.
Born November 30, 1949. Height 5 ft. 11½ in. Weight 11 st. 4 lb.

STEVE MELNYK (U.S.)

This man made a fantastic impact on the amateur game on both sides of the Atlantic, but has found U.S. tour life very tough. As an amateur he held the U.S. amateur title in 1969 and the British amateur in 1971. He also made two appearances in the Walker Cup. As a pro, his best 1971 show was to finish fifth in Jacksonville. Since then he has been working steadily and has been rewarded, in 1973, with a share of second place at Phoenix.
Born February 26, 1947. Height 6 ft. 1½ in. Weight 225 lb.

JOHNNY MILLER (U.S.)

As an amateur finished eighth in the 1966 U.S. Open and it was not long before he was drawn towards the professional ranks, making his début in 1969. In three years he has won £90,000 with two major titles, the Southern in 1971 and the Heritage in 1972. In 1971 he also finished second in the Masters (with Jack Nicklaus) and third in the Jacksonville Open, where he three-putted the last green. In early 1973 he finished equal second on two occasions.
Born April 29, 1947. Height 6 ft. 2 in. Weight 175 lb.

197

ORVILLE MOODY (U.S.)

Orville Moody did not qualify for the U.S. tour until 1967, by which time he was already 34. But it was not long before he became world news. Half-way through his second year he marched off with the U.S. Open title and won the World Series of Golf. Since then, however, he has found winning on tour a little more difficult. Early 1973 showed a change of fortunes as he took second place in the Crosby and Hawaiian. *Born December 9, 1933. Height 5 ft. 10 in. Weight 200 lb.*

BOB MURPHY (U.S.)

Won the Philadelphia and Thunderbird Opens on successive weekends in 1968 and thoroughly earned the "Rookie-of-the-Year" title – as well as 10th spot in the money-winners' list. He dropped back in 1969 but, taking the Hartford in 1970, he was back to ninth place with some £45,000 in the bank. The year 1971 was again disappointing, the nearest to success being third in the Crosby National, Houston Champions and the American Golf Classic. He was also tied fourth in the Monsanto Open. In 1972 he had one second on the U.S. tour before travelling to Australia to win their Masters title. In early 1973 he finished second in the Gleason Classic and the Tallahassee Open. *Born February 14, 1943. Height 5 ft. 10 in. Weight 215 lb.*

HEDLEY MUSCROFT (U.K.)

A professional since 1954, his first big success came in 1968 with a win in the Evian Open. Same year he finished third in the Alcan International Championship and 11th in the P.G.A. Order of Merit. In 1970 he won the Classic International and finished third (with Lionel Platts) in the Sumrie Better-ball tournament. He has three victories in the Yorkshire Open and three in the Yorkshire Professional Championship. He slipped from 25th to 44th in the Order of Merit last year, but came back in 1973 with a semi-final shot in the Benson and Hedges Match-play. *Born April 3, 1938. Height 6 ft. 1 in. Weight 15 st.*

198

KEL NAGLE (Australia)

Holder of the 1971 World Seniors' Championship, it was way back in 1954 when Nagle first broke into the news. That year, with Peter Thomson as partner, he won the Canada Cup for Australia, a feat they were to repeat in 1959. In 1960 he won the Centenary British Open at St. Andrews. Has also won the Australian Open, Australian-New Zealand Professional Championship, Canadian Open and French Open. Last year he was also successful in the Volvo tournament in Sweden, runner-up in the Martini, fourth in Carrolls International. His most recent success was in the latest New Zealand P.G.A. Championship.

Born December 21, 1920. Height 5 ft. $10\frac{1}{2}$ in. Weight 13 st. 7 lb.

JACK NEWTON (Australia)

The man whom Tony Jacklin rates "the best prospect I have seen outside America" had back-to-back victories in the Dutch Open and the Benson and Hedges Festival and, in all, finished in the top 10 on eight occasions. It helped put him in fifth position in the Order of Merit table. He returned to Australia and then played in the New Zealand circuit where he won the City of Auckland title and also took one second and two thirds.

Born January 30, 1950. Height 5 ft. 11 in. Weight 12 st. 8 lb.

BOBBY NICHOLS (U.S.)

Consistent performer in the big events, and since 1962 has won nine top titles. These include the P.G.A. Championship (1964), Carling World Open (1964), P.G.A. Team (1968), Houston (1962, 1965). He missed the 1967 Masters by one shot and in same year was named for the U.S. Ryder Cup team. The year 1971 did not see a win, but out of 27 events he was placed in the top 10 on seven occasions, headed by a second place in the Western. He returned 34 rounds under 70, and in seven tournaments never had a round over par. In 1972 he included a second and two thirds in a consistent season.

Born April 14, 1936. Height 6 ft. 2 in. Weight 198 lb.

CHRISTY O'CONNOR (U.K.)

A dominating personality in British golf for 16 years he has won more official money than any other player on the circuit. Has recorded successes in Daks (1959), Irish Hospitals (1960, 1962), Martini (1963 tie and 1964), Senior Service (1965), Alcan International (1968 tie), Dunlop Masters (1956, 1959), P.G.A. Match-play Championship (1957), four wins in the Carrolls International and three in the Gallaher Ulster Open, John Player Classic (1970). Has represented Britain in every Ryder Cup match since 1955, and played 14 times for Ireland in the World Cup. Last year he finished 14th in the Order of Merit.

Born December 21, 1924. Height 5 ft. 10 in. Weight 13 st. 6½ lb.

JOHN O'LEARY (U.K.)

One of Ireland's most outstanding prospects since turning professional in 1971. In his first season on tour he finished 97th in the Order of Merit. Last year he raced up the table to 32nd, thanks to several fine showings. His best were joint fifth in the Benson and Hedges Match-play and the Dunlop Masters. In South Africa, where he plays tournament golf during the winter, he was pipped for their 1972 Masters title at the last hole. Gary Player was the winner.

Born August 19, 1949. Height 6 ft. 2 in. Weight 14 st. 7 lb.

ARNOLD PALMER (U.S.)

There is enough to say statistically about him to fill 20 pages of this book. He has won over 60 major titles – everything bar the U.S.P.G.A. – and it was not until 1970 that he went a year without a U.S. tour victory. He returned with a bang in 1971, with four wins and third place in the U.S. money-winners' list. The year 1972 was another dismal one with no wins and a drop to 25th in the money list. Early 1973 saw a return to the winner's enclosure when he recorded five sub-par rounds to take the Hope Classic title.

Born September 10, 1929. Height 5 ft. 10½ in. Weight 185 lb.

LIONEL PLATTS (U.K.)

First came into prominence in 1964 with success in the Braemar tournament and a final seventh place in the P.G.A. Order of Merit. The following year he lost a play-off in the Swallow-Penfold, lost to Neil Coles in the final of the P.G.A. Match-play Championship, and lost in a three-way play-off for the Gallaher Ulster Open. A place in the Ryder Cup team was some consolation. Last year won the Portuguese Open and finished in 13th place in the Order of Merit.
Born October 10, 1934. Height 6 ft. Weight 14 st. 7 lb.

GARY PLAYER (South Africa)

Among his most important titles are two Open Championships, one U.S. Open title, one U.S. Masters title, two U.S.P.G.A. titles, eight South African Open titles, six Australian Open titles and four Piccadilly World Match-play titles. In 1972 he had a fine season everywhere but in Europe. He won the South African Open, the New Orleans Open, the U.S.P.G.A. Championship, the Japan Airlines Open and the Brazilian Open. Early in 1973 he had to have a serious operation, but was soon back on the circuits of the world.
Born November 1, 1936. Height 5 ft. 8 in. Weight 11 st. 5 lb.

EDDIE POLLAND (U.K.)

At 18, runner-up in the Irish Boys' Championship and one year later he joined the professional ranks. In 1970 won the Irish Assistants' Championship and was runner-up to Peter Oosterhuis in the Coca-Cola Young Professionals' Championship. Three Irish tournaments fell to him in 1971. Last year saw him leap to 28th in the Order of Merit with joint fourth in the Carrolls as his best showing. Early in 1973 he achieved his first victory in the Penfold-Bournemouth.
Born June 10, 1947. Height 5 ft. 11 in. Weight 11 st. 7 lb.

201

DAI REES (U.K.)

Can lay claim to more major tournament successes than any other British golfer at present playing. His first success came in 1936 when winning the *News of the World* Match-play, which he also won in 1938, 1949 and 1950. He has recorded two wins in the Dunlop Masters, and held the Harry Vardon Trophy twice. Has played for Britain nine times in the Ryder Cup, four times as captain (once non-playing captain), and led Britain to victory in 1957. Awarded a C.B.E. for services to golf, his appetite for the game seems insatiable. In 1971, at 58 years of age, he played in 15 P.G.A. tournaments for an average of 73·26 per round. Has represented Wales eight times in World Cup matches, and led his country during the Double Diamond Home International series.
Born March 31, 1913. Height 5 ft. 7 in. Weight 11 st. 7 lb.

DOUG SANDERS (U.S.)

Well known for his exploits at the British Open, he became a top U.S. tour man a year after turning pro in 1957. He has won 19 events up to the end of last year. Best year was 1961, when he won five events. In 1971 he slipped back to 85th in the money order, with a tied 11th place his best of the year. Last year he recaptured form, winning the Kemper Open on his way up to 16th among the money-winners.
Born July 24, 1933. Height 5 ft. 11 in. Weight 165 lb.

JOHN SCHLEE (U.S.)

Named Rookie-of-the-Year after finishing 47th in the 1966 money-winners' list, he has never improved on that position and was out of the top 60 every year from then until 1971. That year six finishes in the top 10, including a tie for seventh in San Diego and a tie for eighth in Hawaii, helped him earn nearly $50,000. His big break came in 1973 when he recorded his first tour victory in Hawaii.
Born June 2, 1939. Height 6 ft. 3 in. Weight 170 lb.

202

RONNIE SHADE (U.K.)

A professional since 1968, he won the Ben Sayers tournament in 1969, followed by success in Carrolls International. That year saw him 20th in the P.G.A. Order of Merit. Took the Scottish P.G.A. Championship in 1970, was runner-up in the Long John Scotch Whisky Match-play Championship, just failed to retain the Carrolls title, but moved up to 14th final placing. Dropped back to 29th in 1971 and 43rd last year when his best show, was third in the Benson and Hedges Match-play.

Born October 15, 1938. Height 5 ft. 11 in. Weight 11 st. 3 lb.

DAN SIKES (U.S.)

Joining the tour when 29, he has won six events, the peak money-winning list period being in 1967 (5th) and 1968 (8th). During those two years, the Jacksonville, Philadelphia, Florida Citrus and Minnesota titles came his way. The years 1970 and 1971 were not so productive, but second place in the Phoenix in 1971 restored a little confidence. During his Army career he won the All-Army Championship and just before becoming a professional he won the U.S. Public Links Championship. In 1972 he finished 61st in the money-winners' list.

Born December 7, 1930. Height 6 ft. 1 in. Weight 185 lb.

J. C. SNEAD (U.S.)

Starting his professional life in 1964, it was four years later before a venture was made on to the tour. But 1971 saw a startling change. Within the space of three weeks two big titles were in the bag. First came the Tucson with a final round of 66, and two weeks later 66 and 69 final rounds brought in the Doral title. He had four more top 10 finishes, including a second in the Hartford. In 1972 he dropped to 22nd from 17th in the money-winners' list with one win – in Philadelphia. The year 1973 saw a further leap towards stardom when he failed to land the Masters by one shot.

Born October 14, 1941. Height 6 ft. 2 in. Weight 205 lb.

203

SAM SNEAD (U.S.)

Now 61, he has become something of a legend in his playing life. His list of honours is enormous, but suffice it to say he was U.S.P.G.A. champion three times, U.S. Masters champion three times, the winner of 84 P.G.A. co-sponsored events, Vardon Trophy winner four times and a Ryder Cup player eight times. In 1972 he was 71st in the money-winners' list, earning around £5,000 more than the previous year. Currently, he holds the U.S. Seniors title.
Born May 27, 1912. Height 5 ft. 11 in. Weight 195 lb.

RAMON SOTA (Spain)

Three Open Championships in 1971, the Algarve Open, put him firmly in the No. 1 spot in Europe. Having won the Portuguese Open towards the end of 1970, Sota was at the beginning of a successful streak which also included second in the Italian B.P. Open, third in the Spanish Open, fourth in the Madrid Open. A leading player for 12 years, he has been four times Spanish Professional Champion, winner of the French Open as well as the Championships of Puerto Rico and Madrid. His 1972 season was a poor one with his best tour performance being joint 20th in the Lancia d'Ovo.
Born April 23, 1938. Height 5 ft. 7 in. Weight 12 st. 10 lb.

DAVE STOCKTON (U.S.)

A remarkably consistent performer, one who rarely makes news, but is always very high up in the lists. In just nine years as a professional he has won £180,000 and six tournaments. These include the P.G.A. Championship in 1971, the Cleveland, Milwaukee, and last year the Massachusetts. The year 1971 saw a somewhat shortened programme of events, but in 27 starts Stockton was in the money 24 times, in the top 10 six times, to finish 19th in the money-winners' list. He slipped to 30th with two thirds as best placing in 1972. In early 1973 he finished runner-up in Houston.
Born November 2, 1941. Height 5 ft. 11½ in. Weight 180 lb.

PETER THOMSON (Australia)

Australia's leading golfer for something like 20 years, this man has won virtually every honour in the game outside America, which he has seldom visited. He has won more than 60 major titles, including the Open – five times! He has also been Australian Open champion three times, the final one coming last year, and New Zealand Open champion on nine occasions. Last season, on a short trip to Britain he won the Wills Open and then had two victories in Japan.
Born August 23, 1929. Height 5 ft. 9½ in. Weight 12 st. 2 lb.

SAM TORRANCE (U.K.)

Named Britain's 1972 Rookie-of-the-Year, he burst on the professional scene in exciting fashion. He became Under-25 Match-play champion, including Bernard Gallacher and Doug McClelland among his victims, won the unofficial Radici Open in Italy, finished joint seventh in the Player Trophy and joint 11th in the Masters. All this helped lift him to 37th in the Order of Merit list.
Born August 24th, 1953. Height 6 ft. Weight 13 st. 7 lb.

PETER TOWNSEND (U.K.)

Has won seven major titles and represented Britain in the 1969 and 1971 Ryder Cup matches. His only win in 1967 was the Dutch Open, but he followed with a brilliant year in 1968, winning the Piccadilly P.G.A. Championship and the Coca-Cola in Britain and the Western Australian Open. He was also second to defending champion Gay Brewer in the Alcan Golfer of the Year Championship at Royal Birkdale. He spent most of 1969–70 on the U.S. circuit without a win. Returning to Europe in 1971 he won the Swiss Open and the Walworth-Aloyco in Italy, and finished third in the Spanish Open, third in the Daks and fifth in the Dunlop Masters. Last year he won the Los Lagartos Open and had five finishes in the top 10 on the P.G.A. tour to finish eighth in the Order of Merit.
Born September 16, 1946. Height 5 ft. 8½ in. Weight 11 st. 3 lb.

205

PETER TUPLING (U.K.)

A British Boy Champion, member of Walker Cup team, Yorkshire Amateur Champion and leading amateur in the Open Championship for 1969. Joined professional ranks early in 1970. He made an immediate impact with a tie for fourth place in the Daks tournament. In 1971 he shared second place in the W. D. and H. O. Wills Open, with a final round of 69. That year he finished 57th in the Order of Merit, but last year he moved up to 41st, thanks to five finishes in the top 18. Highlight of the year was a first round 68 for the Open lead. He was still in contention for a big cheque after three rounds, but slipped with a final 81.
Born April 6, 1950. Height 6 ft. 2 in. Weight 13 st. 1 lb.

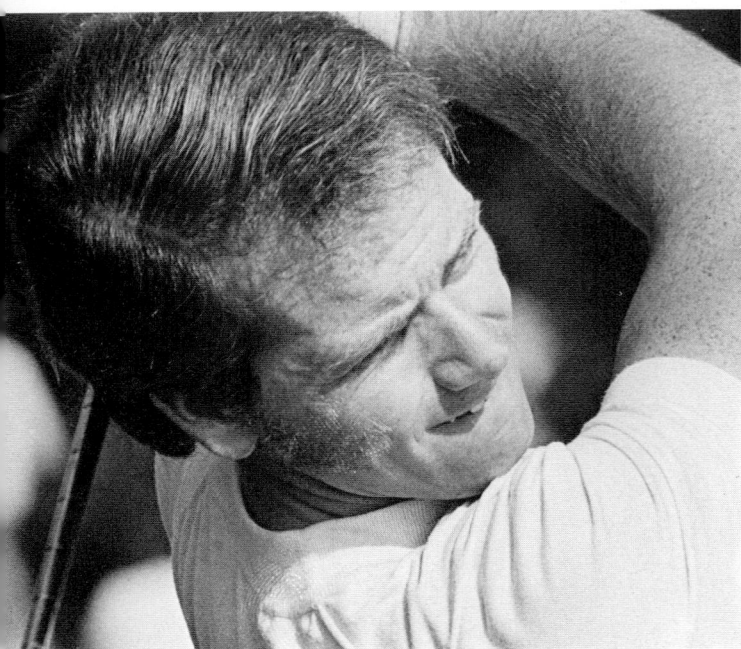

DAVID VAUGHAN (U.K.)

First representative honours in 1971 for Wales in the Double Diamond Home International tournament. This followed a year of consistency with success in Lord Derby's Under-23 Championship and a fourth in the Welsh Open. He finished 26th in the P.G.A. Order of Merit. Improvement continued and he rose to 11th, thanks to a third in the Benson and Hedges, joint fifth in the Piccadilly Medal, joint seventh in the Open and joint eighth in the Dutch Open and the P.G.A. Championship.
Born June 26, 1948. Height 5 ft. 8 in. Weight 10 st. 10 lb.

ROBERTO de VICENZO (Argentina)

A professional since 1940 and something like 130 tournament wins on the record card. And that includes 32 national Opens! Represented Argentina 13 times in World Cup events, has been Champion of that country on seven occasions, won the British Open in 1967, a career highlight, almost won the U.S. Masters in 1968 when he missed a playoff by signing a wrong scorecard, and in 1971 recorded a 69·89 stroke average in eight British and European tournaments. Most recent wins were the Panama Open and the Caracas Open.
Born April 14, 1923. Height 6 ft. 2 in. Weight 12 st. 11 lb.

206

LANNY WADKINS (U.S.)

He won the U.S. amateur title in 1970, playing in the Walker Cup in 1969 and 1971 and the World Amateur championships in 1970. He graduated to the pro scene late in 1971 and immediately sounded a warning by finishing third in the Disney World event. Last year he proved a sensation by winning one event and coming second twice as he moved up to 10th in the money-winners' list. It earned him the Rookie-of-the-Year title. Early in 1973 he proved this was no momentary flash of ability by winning the Byron Nelson, sharing second in Phoenix and third in Houston.

Born December 5, 1949. Height 5 ft. 8½ in. Weight 165 lb.

TERRY WESTBROOK (Rhodesia)

Based in South Africa, he has been one of their top competitors in recent years, winning the Natal Open in 1971 and the Schoeman Park Open last year. He played in 19 events on the P.G.A. tour last season and finished in 50th position. On three occasions he finished in the top 10. He and Australian Vic Bennetts finished joint fourth in the Sumrie Better-Ball event, he was joint fifth in the Dutch Open and joint sixth in the P.G.A. Championship.

Born May 19, 1938. Height 5 ft. 11 in. Weight 13 st. 3 lb.

PETER WILCOCK (U.K.)

Winner of the Northern Young Professionals Championship in 1968 and 1969. Runner-up in the 1970 Daks tournament. That same year he was seventh in the Martini International and 10th in the Gallaher Ulster Open, and ended 24th in the P.G.A. Order of Merit list. In 1971 he qualified for the last round of several major tournaments, finishing 16th in the Classic International and 17th in the German Open. Last year he was Italian B.P. Open Champion, and joint fourth in the Carrolls was his best P.G.A. tour showing. It helped push him into 17th place in the Order of Merit.

Born November 18, 1945. Height 5 ft. 11 in. Weight 11 st.

The British Order of Merit 1972

		POINTS	TNMTS	STROKES	ROUNDS	AVERAGE	PRIZE-MONEY
1	P. Oosterhuis	1751·0	19	4240	60	70·66	£18,525·46
2	G. L. Hunt	1710·0	19	4221	59	71·54	9,808·81
3	B. Huggett	1702·0	19	4304	60	71·73	10,166·88
4	P. Townsend	1639·5	23	5210	72	72·36	8,592·04
5	J. Newton	1636·5	21	4628	64	72·31	8,899·19
6	J. Garner	1616·0	22	4890	67	72·98	8,005·59
7	P. Butler	1613·5	22	4652	64	72·68	8,375·93
8	B. Barnes	1602·5	20	4614	64	72·08	9,103·90
9	N. Coles	1597·0	17	3843	53	72·51	8,629·25
10	C. Clark	1575·0	21	4654	64	72·71	5,831·27
11	D. Vaughan	1565·5	22	4903	67	73·17	5,321·13
12	B. Gallacher	1551·5	23	4972	68	73·11	4,371·65
13	L. Platts	1540·0	22	4678	64	73·09	3,079·45
14	C. O'Connor, Snr.	1510·5	19	—	—	—	6,162·09
15	T. Horton	1504·5	22	5076	69	73·56	5,661·54
16	H. Bannerman	1478·5	17	3797	52	73·01	6,549·79
17	P. Wilcock	1477·0	21	4385	60	73·08	2,411·74
18	H. Baiocchi	1474·5	20	4246	58	73·20	2,937·86
19	M. Bembridge	1450·0	21	4686	64	73·21	3,822·51
20	M. Ballesteros	1442·5	18	4357	60	72·61	2,992·32
21	V. Hood	1425·5	16	3272	45	72·71	2,970·99
22	D. McClelland	1423·5	23	4672	63	74·15	3,426·13
23	B. J. Hunt	1412·5	18	3690	50	73·80	2,933·35
24	M. Gregson	1399·0	17	3650	50	73·00	3,253·16
25	N. Wood	1390·0	18	3681	50	73·62	4,971·82
26	H. Jackson	1372·0	21	4255	58	73·36	2,277·07
27	N. Job	1364·0	21	4437	60	73·95	2,490·17
28	E. Polland	1361·0	23	4689	64	73·26	2,736·43
29	A. Brooks	1348·0	18	3755	51	73·62	1,714·06
30	C. O'Connor, Jnr.	1265·0	20	3626	49	74·00	2,198·63
31	G. Cunningham	1264·5	20	4024	54	74·51	1,441·64
32	J. O'Leary	1255·5	19	—	—	—	2,519·68
33	W. Humphreys	1253·0	22	3831	52	73·67	1,041·86
34	D. Talbot	1250·5	14	3317	45	73·71	3,635·97
35	J. Dorrestein	1248·5	19	4067	55	73·94	1,867·10
36	C. De Foy	1230·5	21	3954	53	74·60	1,657·31
37	S. Torrance	1211·5	20	—	—	—	1,731·94
38	N. C. Hunt	1201·5	21	3964	53	74·79	972·06
39	R. Walker	1189·0	17	—	—	—	1,160·67
40	J. Kinsella	1171·5	18	3266	44	74·22	3,451·30
41	P. Tupling	1108·0	20	3540	48	73·75	1,451·95
42	H. Boyle	1105·0	19	—	—	—	1,293·58
43	R. Shade	1093·0	15	—	—	—	2,953·81
44	H. Muscroft	1090·0	17	—	—	—	1,227·36
45	R. Bernardini	1085·5	12	—	—	—	4,308·79
46	M. Ingham	1085·0	16	—	—	—	1,182·37
47	K. Dabson	1083·5	18	—	—	—	1,024·82
48	D. Swaelens	1078·0	14	3076	42	73·23	1,575·26
49	D. Butler	1070·0	18	3204	43	74·51	723·08
50	T. Westbrook	1037·0	19	2885	39	73·97	1,581·60
51	R. Sota	1032·0	14	3469	47	73·80	1,631·02
52	I. Stanley	1009·5	16	—	—	—	1,054·26
53	V. Baker	992·5	19	2741	37	74·08	761·75
54	W. Murray	987·5	18	3448	46	74·95	1,333·09
55	J. Cook	986·5	20	3335	45	74·11	1,048·35
56	S. Brown	961·0	17	3045	41	74·26	1,217·64
57	A. Gallardo	934·0	12	2750	38	72·36	3,067·17
58	E. Brown	930·5	18	—	—	—	946·50
59	B. Dassu	913·5	15	2921	39	74·89	1,582·78

208

60	D. Small	909·5	16	2226	30	74·20	540·95
61	G. Baleson	904·5	18	3199	43	74·39	1,112·55
62	W. Large	901·0	16	2668	35	76·22	495·67
63	J. Gallardo	899·5	12	2472	34	72·70	2,998·43
64	D. Hayes	878·0	15	—	—	—	2,146·28
65	D. Jones	856·0	19	2497	34	73·44	677·55
66	G. A. Caygill	832·0	16	2461	33	74·57	604·32
67	D. Jagger	822·5	17	3042	41	74·19	1,116·79
68	V. Barrios	818·5	10	—	—	—	2,707·66
69	A. Jacklin	813·0	11	1830	26	70·38	16,225·94
70	A. Phillips	760·5	21	2874	38	75·63	336·66
71	S. Rolley	749·0	16	2375	32	74·21	922·93
72	P. Cowen	727·5	17	2461	33	74·57	637·97
73	J. Panton	726·0	12	2231	30	74·36	890·91
74	D. Webster	702·5	15	2198	29	75·79	395·31
75	D. Llewellyn	696·5	20	2702	36	75·05	1,161·14
76	T. Claassens, S.A.	683·5	16	—	—	—	313·78
77	S. Levermore	654·0	16	—	—	—	489·43
78	C. Baker	651·5	15	2153	29	74·24	454·39
79	D. Huish	640·0	11	1495	20	74·75	1,110·44
80	G. Wolstenholme, Aus.	638·5	9	1960	27	72·59	1,182·60
81	D. Rees	637·0	12	1964	26	75·53	504·83
82	A. Grubb	613·5	11	1721	23	74·82	694·15
83	M. Moussa, U.A.R.	605·5	6	1722	24	71·75	925·25
84	A. Bird	602·0	16	2439	32	76·21	324·69
85	R. Whitehead	594·5	14	1961	26	75·42	2,160·08
86	J. Fowler	587·5	11	2360	32	73·75	645·83
87	T. Lopez, S.	583·5	9	—	—	—	631·20
88	A. Sutton, S.A.	578·0	8	1552	21	73·90	544·88
89	T. Britz, S.A.	577·5	7	1905	26	73·26	877·16
90	R. Charles, NZ.	537·5	6	1349	19	71·00	18,538·75
91	F. Abreu, S.	567·5	7	1676	23	72·86	540·50
92	G. Marsh, Aus.	562·5	5	1407	20	70·35	4,096·33
93	B. Allen	561·5	15	1775	24	73·95	195·53
94	R. Shearer, Aus.	560·0	9	1767	24	73·62	518·01
95	D. Scanlon	558·0	8	1715	23	74·56	340·35
96	K. Robson	539·5	10	1316	18	73·11	779·98
97	J. Canizares, S.	536·5	6	1436	20	71·80	3,190·00
98	M. Walters	534·5	12	1613	21	76·80	212·96
99	R. Fidler	527·0	10	1242	17	73·05	674·75
100	E. Jones	508·5	6	1634	22	74·27	504·88

American Money Standing 1972

1	Jack Nicklaus	$320,542		51	Babe Hiskey	49,490
2	Lee Trevino	214,806		52	Rod Funseth	48,238
3	George Archer	145,027		53	Larry Hinson	48,238
4	Grier Jones	140,178		54	Bob Goalby	47,935
5	Jerry Heard	136,998		55	Jerry McGee	47,551
6	Tom Weiskopf	129,422		56	Brian Allin	47,577
7	Gary Player	120,720		57	Fred Marti	46,270
8	Bruce Devlin	119,768		58	Hubert Green	44,113
9	Tommy Aaron	118,925		59	Ken Still	43,351
10	Lanny Wadkins	116,617		60	Bob E. Smith	43,297
11	Bob Mitchell	113,719		61	Dan Sikes	42,139
12	Juan Rodriguez	113,449		62	Mac McLendon	40,251
13	Hale Irwin	111,530		63	Leonard Thompson	39,882
14	Bruce Crampton	111,010		64	Chris Blocker	38,463
15	Jim Jamieson	109,533		65	George Johnson	38,454
16	Doug Sanders	102,253		66	Art Wall, Jr.	38,218
17	John Miller	99,349		67	Dave Eichelberger	37,543
18	Dave Hill	98,464		68	Larry Ziegler	36,864
19	Lou Graham	96,078		69	Don Iverson	35,715
20	Homero Blancas	93,019		70	Ray Floyd	35,624
21	Deane Beman	88,859		71	Sam Snead	35,463
22	J. C. Snead	87,435		72	Dwight Nevil	35,385
23	Jim Colbert	85,302		73	Gibby Gilbert	34,200
24	Gay Brewer	84,313		74	Dale Douglass	33,146
25	Arnold Palmer	84,181		75	Cesar Sanudo	33,072
26	Bob Murphy	83,260		76	Charles Sifford	32,616
27	Bob Rosburg	78,887		77	Steve Melnyk	31,435
28	Bob Nichols	78,297		78	Larry Wood	31,336
29	Bert Yancey	75,927		79	Tom Watson	31,081
30	George Knudson	74,336		80	Al Geiberger	29,710
31	Miller Barber	73,664		81	Marty Fleckman	28,601
32	Lee Elder	70,402		82	Tom Shaw	27,975
33	Mike Hill	67,068		83	John Schroeder	27,797
34	Dave Stockton	66,112		84	Tom Ulozas	27,568
35	Tony Jacklin	65,976		85	Ron Cerrudo	27,349
36	Labron Harris	64,909		86	Mason Rudolph	27,345
37	Charles Coody	62,505		87	Ralph Johnston	26,560
38	David Graham	57,827		88	Forest Fezier	26,543
39	John Mahaffey	57,779		89	Don January	25,833
40	Frank Beard	56,188		90	Julius Boros	25,774
41	Billy Casper	55,476		91	Bob Shaw	25,184
42	Jim Wiechers	54,749		92	Chuck Thorpe	25,165
43	Don Bies	54,452		93	Jim Dent	24,285
44	Kermit Zarley	54,134		94	John Lister	24,173
45	Phil Rodgers	53,512		95	Bert Greene	23,298
46	DeWitt Weaver	53,279		96	John Jacobs	22,972
47	Chuck Courtney	52,264		97	Bob Charles	21,809
48	Paul Harney	51,508		98	Bunky Henry	21,703
49	John Schlee	51,236		99	Dave Marad	21,013
50	Bob Lunn	51,114		100	Sam Adams	20,747

British Tournament Winners 1972

DATE	PURSE	TOURNAMENT	WINNER	PRIZE-MONEY
April 24–29	£12,000	Piccadilly Medal	T. Horton	£2,437
May 11–13	8,000	Penfold-Bournemouth	P. Oosterhuis	1,462
May 17–20	8,000	Sumrie	B. Huggett/ M. Gregson	780
May 25–27	8,000	John Player Trophy	R. Whitehead	1,463
June 1–3	4,000	Coca-Cola Young Pros	P. Oosterhuis	585
June 8–10	8,000	Martini	B. Barnes	1,462
June 20–22	2,750	Pringle Seniors	K. Bousfield	500
June 22–25	15,000	Carrolls	C. O'Connor	2,437
June 28–July 1	10,000	Scottish Open	N. Coles	1,950
July 12–15	50,000	The Open	L. Trevino	5,500
Aug 16–19	15,000	Benson and Hedges Festival	J. Newton	2,193
Aug 23–26	15,000	Vigella P.G.A.	A. Jacklin	2,193
Sept 13–16	20,000	Benson and Hedges Match-play	J. Garner	3,412
Sept 20–23	15,000	Wills Open	P. Thomson	2,193
Sept 27–30	56,550	Player Classic	R. Charles	14,625
Oct 4–7	15,000	Dunlop Masters	R. Charles	1,950
Oct 12–14	25,000	Piccadilly World Match-play Championship	T. Weiskopf	8,287

Bob Charles

Neil Coles

Peter Oosterhuis

Christy O'Connor

American Tournament Winners 1972

DATE	PURSE	TOURNAMENT	WINNER	PRIZE-MONEY
Jan 6–9	$125,000	Los Angeles Open	G. Archer	$25,000
Jan 13–16	140,000	Crosby Pro-Am	J. Nicklaus	28,000
Jan 20–23	150,000	Tucson Open	M. Barber	30,000
Jan 27–30	150,000	San Diego Open	P. Harney	30,000
Feb 3–6	200,000	Hawaiian Open	G. Jones	40,000
Feb 9–13	145,000	Desert Classic	R. Rosburg	29,000
Feb 17–20	125,000	Phoenix Open	H. Blancas	25,000
Feb 24, 27	260,000	Inverrary Classic	T. Weiskopf	52,000
Mar 2–6	150,000	Doral-Eastern Open	J. Nicklaus	30,000
Mar 9–12	150,000	Florida Citrus Open	J. Heard	30,000
Mar 16–19	125,000	Gr. Jacksonville Open	A. Jacklin	25,000
Mar 23–26	125,000	Gr. New Orleans Open	G. Player	25,000
Mar 30–Apr 2	190,000	Gr. Greensboro Open	G. Archer	40,000
Apr 6–9	204,649	U.S. Masters	J. Nicklaus	25,000
Apr 13–16	150,000	Monsanto Open	D. Hill	20,000
Apr 20–23	165,000	Tournament of Champions	B. Mitchell	33,000
Apr 20–23	75,000	Tallahassee Open	B. Shaw	15,000
Apr 27–May 1	125,000	Byron Nelson Classic	J. Rodriguez	25,000
May 4–7	125,000	Houston Open	B. Devlin	25,000
May 11–14	125,000	Colonial National	J. Heard	25,000
May 18–21	175,000	Memphis Classic	L. Trevino	35,000
May 25–28	130,000	Atlanta Classic	R. Lunn	26,000
June 1–4	175,000	Kemper Open	D. Sanders	35,000
June 8–11	150,000	IVB-Philadelphia Classic	J. C. Snead	30,000
June 15–18	200,000	U.S. Open	J. Nicklaus	30,000
June 22–25	150,000	Western Open	J. Jamieson	30,000
June 29–July 2	150,000	Cleveland Open	D. Graham	30,000
July 6–9	150,000	Canadian Open	G. Brewer	30,000
July 13–16	125,000	Great Milwaukee Open	J. Colbert	25,000
July 20–23	150,000	American Classic	B. Yancey	30,000
July 27–30	200,000	National Team Chp.	B. Hiskey/K. Zarley	20,000
Aug 3–6	225,000	U.S.P.G.A.	G. Player	45,000
Aug 10–13	250,000	Westchester Classic	J. Nicklaus	50,000
Aug 17–20	200,000	U.S. Inter. Classic	B. Devlin	40,000
Aug 24–27	100,000	Liggett and Myers Open	L. Graham	20,000
Aug 26–27	150,000	U.S. Pro Match-play	J. Nicklaus	40,000
Sept 1–4	125,000	Gt. Hartford Open	L. Trevino	25,000
Sept 7–10	100,000	Southern Open	D. Weaver	20,000
Sept 9–10	77,500	World Series	G. Player	50,000
Sept 14–17	150,000	St. Louis Classic	L. Trevino	30,000
Sept 21–24	100,000	Robinson Fall Classic	G. Jones	20,000
Sept 28–Oct 1	100,000	Quad Cities Open	D. Beman	20,000
Oct 19–22	150,000	Kaiser Open	G. Knudson	30,000
Oct 26–29	135,000	Sahara Invitational	L. Wadkins	27,000
Nov 2–5	125,000	Texas Open	M. Hill	25,000
Nov 23–27	125,000	Heritage Classic	J. Miller	25,000
Nov 30–Dec 3	150,000	Disney World Open	J. Nicklaus	30,000

Open Championship

THE BELT

YEAR	WINNER	VENUE	SCORE
1860	W. Park, Musselburgh	Prestwick	174
1861	Tom Morris, Snr., Prestwick	Prestwick	163
1862	Tom Morris, Snr., Prestwick	Prestwick	163
1863	W. Park, Musselburgh	Prestwick	168
1864	Tom Morris, Snr., Prestwick	Prestwick	167
1865	A. Strath, St. Andrews	Prestwick	162
1866	W. Park, Musselburgh	Prestwick	169
1867	Tom Morris, Snr., St. Andrews	Prestwick	170
1868	Tom Morris, Jnr., St. Andrews	Prestwick	157
1869	Tom Morris, Jnr., St. Andrews	Prestwick	154
1870	Tom Morris, Jnr., St. Andrews	Prestwick	149

THE CUP

YEAR	WINNER	VENUE	SCORE
1872	Tom Morris, Jnr., St. Andrews	Prestwick	166
1873	Tom Kidd, St. Andrews	St. Andrews	179
1874	Mungo Park, Musselburgh	Musselburgh	159
1875	Willie Park, Musselburgh	Prestwick	166
1876	Bob Martin, St. Andrews	St. Andrews	176
	(David Strath tied but refused to play off)		
1877	Jamie Anderson, St. Andrews	Musselburgh	160
1878	Jamie Anderson, St. Andrews	Prestwick	157
1879	Jamie Anderson, St. Andrews	St. Andrews	170
1880	Bob Ferguson, Musselburgh	Musselburgh	162
1881	Bob Ferguson, Musselburgh	Prestwick	170
1882	Bob Ferguson, Musselburgh	St. Andrews	171
1883	W. Fernie, Dumfries	Musselburgh	159
	After a tie with Bob Ferguson, Musselburgh		
1884	Jack Simpson, Carnoustie	Prestwick	160
1885	Bob Martin, St. Andrews	St. Andrews	171
1886	D. Brown, Musselburgh	Musselburgh	157
1887	W. Park, Jnr., Musselburgh	Prestwick	161
1888	Jack Burns, Warwick	St. Andrews	171
1889	W. Park, Jnr., Musselburgh	Musselburgh	155
	After a tie with Andrew Kirkaldy		
1890	Mr. John Ball, Royal Liverpool	Prestwick	164
1891	Hugh Kirkaldy, St. Andrews	St. Andrews	166
	After 1891 the competition was extended to 72 holes and for the first time entry money was imposed		
1892	Mr. H. H. Hilton, Royal Liverpool	Muirfield	305
1893	W. Auchterlonie, St. Andrews	Prestwick	322
1894	J. H. Taylor, Winchester	Sandwich	326
1895	J. H. Taylor, Winchester	St. Andrews	322
1896	H. Vardon, Ganton	Muirfield	316
	After a tie with J. H. Taylor. Replay scores for 36 holes: Vardon, 157; Taylor, 161		
1897	Mr. H. H. Hilton, Royal Liverpool	Hoylake	314
1898	H. Vardon, Ganton	Prestwick	307
1899	H. Vardon, Ganton	Sandwich	310
1900	J. H. Taylor, Mid-Surrey	St. Andrews	309
1901	James Braid, Romford	Muirfield	309
1902	Alex Herd, Huddersfield	Hoylake	307
1903	H. Vardon, Totteridge	Prestwick	300
1904	Jack White, Sunningdale	Sandwich	296
1905	James Braid, Walton Heath	St. Andrews	318
1906	James Braid, Walton Heath	Muirfield	300
1907	Arnaud Massy, La Boulie	Hoylake	312
1908	James Braid, Walton Heath	Prestwick	291
1909	J. H. Taylor, Mid-Surrey	Deal	295
1910	James Braid, Walton Heath	St. Andrews	299
1911	Harry Vardon, Totteridge	Sandwich	303
1912	E. Ray, Oxhey	Muirfield	295

Open Championship – continued

YEAR	WINNER	VENUE	SCORE
1913	**J. H. Taylor, Mid-Surrey**	Hoylake	304
1914	**Harry Vardon, Totteridge**	Prestwick	306
1920	**George Duncan, Hanger Hill**	Deal	303
1921	**Jock Hutchison, Glenview, Chicago**	St. Andrews	296

After a tie with Mr. R. H. Wethered, Royal and Ancient. Replay scores: Jock Hutchison 150, Mr. R. H. Wethered 159

1922	**Walter Hagen, Detroit, U.S.A.**	Sandwich	300
1923	**A. G. Havers, Coombe Hill**	Troon	295
1924	**Walter Hagen, Detroit, U.S.A.**	Hoylake	301
1925	**Jim Barnes, U.S.A.**	Prestwick	300
1926	**Mr. R. T. Jones, U.S.A.**	Royal Lytham and St. Annes	291
1927	**Mr. R. T. Jones, U.S.A.**	St. Andrews	285
1928	**Walter Hagen, U.S.A.**	Sandwich	292
1929	**Walter Hagen, U.S.A.**	Muirfield	292
1930	**Mr. R. T. Jones, U.S.A.**	Hoylake	291
1931	**T. D. Armour, U.S.A.**	Carnoustie	296
1932	**G. Sarazen, U.S.A.**	Prince's, Sandwich	283
1933	**D. Shute, U.S.A.**	St. Andrews	292

After a tie with Craig Wood, U.S.A. Replay scores: D. Shute, 149, Craig Wood, 154

1934	**T. H. Cotton, Waterloo, Belgium**	Sandwich	283
1935	**A. Perry, Leatherhead**	Muirfield	283
1936	**A. H. Padgham, Sundridge Park**	Hoylake	287
1937	**T. H. Cotton, Ashridge**	Carnoustie	290
1938	**R. A. Whitcombe, Parkstone**	Sandwich	295
1939	**R. Burton, Sale**	St. Andrews	290
1946	**S. Snead, U.S.A.**	St. Andrews	290
1947	**Fred Daly, Balmoral**	Hoylake	293
1948	**T. H. Cotton, Royal Mid-Surrey**	Muirfield	284
1949	**A. D. Locke, South Africa**	Sandwich	283

After a tie with Harry Bradshaw, Kilcroney. Replay scores: Locke, 135; Bradshaw, 147

1950	**A. D. Locke, South Africa**	Troon	279
1951	**M. Faulkner, unattached**	Portrush	285
1952	**A. D. Locke, South Africa**	Royal Lytham and St. Annes	287
1953	**Ben Hogan, U.S.A.**	Carnoustie	282
1954	**P. W. Thomson, Australia**	Royal Birkdale	283
1955	**P. W. Thomson, Australia**	St. Andrews	281
1956	**P. W. Thomson, Australia**	Hoylake	286
1957	**A. D. Locke, South Africa**	St. Andrews	279
1958	**P. W. Thomson, Australia**	Royal Lytham and St. Annes	278

After a tie with D. C. Thomas, Sudbury. Replay scores: Thomson, 139; Thomas, 143

1959	**G. J. Player, South Africa**	Muirfield	284
1960	**K. D. G. Nagle, Australia**	St. Andrews	278
1961	**Arnold Palmer, U.S.A.**	Royal Birkdale	284
1962	**Arnold Palmer, U.S.A.**	Troon	276
1963	**R. J. Charles, New Zealand**	Royal Lytham and St. Annes	277

After a tie with Phil Rodgers, U.S.A. Replay scores: Charles, 140; Rodgers, 148

1964	**Tony Lema, U.S.A.**	St. Andrews	279
1965	**P. W. Thomson, Australia**	Royal Birkdale	285
1966	**J. Nicklaus, U.S.A.**	Muirfield	282
1967	**R. de Vicenzo, Argentina**	Holylake	278
1968	**G. J. Player, South Africa**	Carnoustie	289
1969	**A. Jacklin, Potters Bar**	Royal Lytham and St. Annes	280
1970	**J. Nicklaus, U.S.A.**	St. Andrews	283

After a tie with D. Sanders. Replay scores: Nicklaus, 72; Sanders, 73

1971	**L. Trevino, U.S.A.**	Royal Birkdale	278
1972	**L. Trevino, U.S.A.**	Muirfield	278
1973	**T. Weiskopf, U.S.A.**	Troon	276

214

The American Open

YEAR	WINNER	VENUE	SCORE
1894	**Willie Dunn, Shinnecock Hills**	New York	Defeated Willie Campbell 2 holes
1895	**H. J. Rawlins, Newport**	Newport	173
1896	**J. Foulis, Chicago**	Southampton	173
1897	**J. Lloyd, Essex**	Wheaton, Ill.	162
1898	**Fred Herd, Chicago**	Shinnecock Hills	328
1899	**W. Smith, Chicago**	Baltimore	315
1900	**Harry Vardon, Ganton**	Wheaton, Ill.	313
1901	**W. Anderson, Pittsfield**	Myopia, Mass.	315
1902	**L. Auchterlonie, Glenview**	Garden City	305
1903	**W. Anderson, Apawamis**	Baltusrol	307
1904	**W. Anderson, Apawamis**	Glenview	304
1905	**W. Anderson, Apawamis**	Myopia	335
1906	**Alex. Smith, Nassau**	Onwentsia	291
1907	**Alex. Ross, Brae Burn**	Chestnut Hill, Pa.	302
1908	**Fred M'Leod, Midlothian**	Myopia, Mass.	322
1909	**Geo. Sargent, Hyde Manor**	Englewood, N.J.	290
1910	**Alex. Smith, Wykagyl**	Philadelphia	289
1911	**J. J. M'Dermott, Philadelphia**	Wheaton, Ill.	307
1912	**J. J. M'Dermott, Atlantic City**	Buffalo, N.Y.	294
1913	**Mr. F. Ouimet, Woodland**	Brookline, Mass.	304
1914	**Walter Hagen, Rochester**	Midlothian	297
1915	**Mr. J. D. Travers, Montclair**	Baltusrol	290
1916	**Mr. Charles Evans, Edgewater**	Minneapolis	286
1919	**Walter Hagen, Rochester**	Braeburn	301
1920	**E. Ray, Oxhey**	Inverness	295
1921	**Jim Barnes, Pelham**	Washington	289
1922	**G. Sarazen, Titusville**	Glencoe	288
1923	**Mr. R. T. Jones, Atlanta**	Inwood, L. I.	296
1924	**Cyril Walker, Englewood**	Oakland Hills	297
1925	**Wm. MacFarlane, Oak Ridge**	Worcester	291
1926	**Mr. R. T. Jones, Atlanta**	Scioto	293
1927	**T. D. Armour, Congressional**	Oakmont	301
1928	**J. Farrell, Quaker Ridge**	Olympia Fields	294
1929	**Mr. R. T. Jones, Atlanta**	Winged Foot, New York	294
1930	**Mr. R. T. Jones, Atlanta**	Interlachen	287
1931	**B. Burke, Round Hill**	Inverness	292
1932	**G. Sarazen, Lakeville**	Fresh Meadow	286
1933	**Mr. J. Goodman, Omaha**	North Shore	287
1934	**O. Dutra, Brentwood Heights**	Merion	293
1935	**S. Parks, South Hills**	Oakmont	299
1936	**T. Manero, Greensboro**	Springfield	282
1937	**R. Guidahi, Beverley Hills**	Oaklands Hills	281
1938	**R. Guldahl, Madison**	Cherry Hills	284
1939	**Byron Nelson, Reading, Pa.**	Philadelphia	284
1940	**W. Lawson Little**	Canterbury, Ohio	287
1941	**Craig Wood, Winged Foot**	Forth Worth, Texas	284
1946	**Lloyd Mangrum**	Canterbury	284
1947	**Lew Worsham, Oakmount**	St. Louis	282
1948	**Ben Hogan, Hershey, Pa.**	Los Angeles	276
1949	**Dr. Cary Middlecoff, Memphis**	Medinah, Ill.	286
1950	**Ben Hogan, Hershey, Pa.**	Merion, Pa.	287
1951	**Ben Hogan, Hershey, Pa.**	Oakland Hills, Mich.	287
1952	**Julius Boros, Southern Pines, N.C.**	Dallas, Texas	281
1953	**Ben Hogan, Hershey, Pa.**	Oakmont	283
1954	**Ed. Furgol, Clayton, Mo.**	Baltusrol	284
1955	**J. Fleck, Davenport, Iowa**	San Francisco	287
1956	**Dr. Cary Middlecoff, Dallas**	Rochester	281

The American Open – continued

YEAR	WINNER	VENUE	SCORE
1957	**Dick Mayer, Florida**	Inverness	282
1958	**Tommy Bolt, Paradise, Fla.**	Tulsa, Okla.	283
1959	**W. Casper, California**	Mamaroneck	282
1960	**Arnold Palmer, Latrobe, Pa.**	Denver, Col.	280
1961	**Gene Littler**	Birmingham, Mich.	281
1962	**J. W. Nicklaus**	Oakmount	283
1963	**Julius Boros**	Brookline, Mass.	293
1964	**Ken Venturi**	Washington	278
1965	**Gary Player, South Africa**	St. Louis	282
1966	**W. Casper, California**	San Francisco	278
1967	**J. W. Nicklaus**	Baltusrol	275
1968	**Lee Trevino**	Rochester	275
1969	**Orville Moody**	Houston, Texas	281
1970	**A. Jacklin, Britain**	Chaska, Minn.	281
1971	**L. Trevino**	Merion, Pa.	280
1972	**J. Nicklaus**	Pebble Beach, Calif.	290
1973	**J. Miller**	Oakmont	279

American Masters

YEAR	WINNER	SCORE	YEAR	WINNER	SCORE
1934	**Horton Smith**	284	1955	**Cary Middlecoff**	279
1935	**Gene Sarazen**	282	1956	**Jack Burke, Jnr.**	289
1936	**Horton Smith**	285	1957	**Doug Ford**	283
1937	**Byron Nelson**	283	1958	**Arnold Palmer**	284
1938	**Henry Picard**	285	1959	**Art Wall, Jnr.**	284
1939	**Ralph Guldahl**	279	1960	**Arnold Palmer**	282
1940	**Jimmy Demaret**	280	1961	**Gary Player**	280
1941	**Craig Wood**	280	1962	**Arnold Palmer**	280
1942	**Byron Nelson**	280	1963	**Jack Nicklaus**	286
1946	**Herman Keiser**	282	1964	**Arnold Palmer**	276
1947	**Jimmy Demaret**	281	1965	**Jack Nicklaus**	271
1948	**Claude Harmon**	279	1966	**Jack Nicklaus**	288
1949	**Sam Snead**	282	1967	**Gay Brewer**	280
1950	**Jimmy Demaret**	283	1968	**Bob Goalby**	277
1951	**Ben Hogan**	280	1969	**George Archer**	281
1952	**Sam Snead**	286	1970	**Billy Casper**	279
1953	**Ben Hogan**	274	1971	**Charles Coody**	279
1954	**Sam Snead**	289	1972	**Jack Nicklaus**	286
			1973	**Tommy Aaron**	283

American P.G.A.

YEAR	WINNER	RUNNER-UP	VENUE	SCORE
1916	James M. Barnes	Jock Hutchinson	Siwanoy C.C., Bronxville, N.Y.	1 up
1919	James M. Barnes	Fred McLeod	Engineers C.C., Roslyn, L.I., N.Y.	6 & 5
1920	Jock Hutchinson	J. Douglas Edgar	Flossmoor C.C., Flossmore, Ill.	1 up
1921	Walter Hagen	James M. Barnes	Inwood C.C., Far Rockaway, N.Y.	3 & 2
1922	Gene Sarazen	Emmet French	Oakmont C.C., Oakmont, Pa.	4 & 3
1923	Gene Sarazen	Walter Hagen	Pelham C.C., Pelham, N.Y.	1 up
1924	Walter Hagen	James M. Barnes	French Lick C.C., French Lick, Ind.	2 up
1925	Walter Hagen	William Mehlhorn	Olympia Fields, Olympia Fields, Ill.	6 & 5
1926	Walter Hagen	Leo Diegel	Salisbury G.C., Westbury, L.I., N.Y.	5 & 3
1927	Walter Hagen	Joe Turnesa	Cedar Crest C.C., Dallas, Texas	1 up
1928	Leo Diegel	Al Espinosa	Five Farms C.C., Baltimore, Md.	6 & 5
1929	Leo Diegel	Johnny Farrell	Hillcrest C.C., Los Angeles, Calif.	6 & 4
1930	Tommy Armour	Gene Sarazen	Fresh Meadows C.C., Flushing, N.Y.	1 up
1931	Tom Creavy	Denny Shute	Wannamoisett C.C., Rumford, R.I.	2 & 1
1932	Olin Dutra	Frank Walsh	Keller G.C., St. Paul, Minn.	4 & 3
1933	Gene Sarazen	Willie Goggin	Blue Mound C.C., Milwaukee, Wis.	5 & 4
1934	Paul Runyan	Craig Wood	Park C.C., Williamsville, N.Y.	1 up
1935	Johnny Revolta	Tommy Armour	Twin Hills C.C., Oklahoma City, Okla.	5 & 4
1936	Denny Shute	Jimmy Thomson	Pinehurst C.C., Pinehurst, N.C.	3 & 2
1937	Denny Shute	Harold McSpaden	Pittsburgh F.C., Aspinwall, Pa.	8 & 7
1938	Paul Runyan	Sam Snead	Shawnee C.C., Shawnee-on-Delaware, Pa.	8 & 7
1939	Henry Picard	Byron Nelson	Pomonok C.C., Flushing, L.I., N.Y.	1 up
1940	Byron Nelson	Sam Snead	Hershey C.C., Hershey, Pa.	1 up
1941	Vic Ghezzi	Byron Nelson	Cherry Hills C.C., Denver, Colo.	1 up
1942	Sam Snead	Jim Turnesa	Seaview C.C., Atlantic City, N.J.	2 & 1
1944	Bob Hamilton	Byron Nelson	Manito G. & C.C., Spokane, Wash.	1 up
1945	Byron Nelson	Sam Byrd	Morraine C.C., Dayton, Ohio	4 & 3
1946	Ben Hogan	Ed Oliver	Portland G.C., Portland, Ore.	6 & 4
1947	Jim Ferrier	Chick Harbert	Plum Hollow C.C., Detroit, Mich.	2 & 1
1948	Ben Hogan	Mike Turnesa	Norwood Hills C.C., St. Louis, Mo.	7 & 6
1949	Sam Snead	Johnny Palmer	Hermitage C.C., Richmond, Va.	3 & 2
1950	Chandler Harper	Henry Williams, Jnr.	Scioto C.C., Columbus, Ohio	4 & 3
1951	Sam Snead	Walter Burkemo	Oakmont C.C., Oakmont, Pa.	7 & 6
1952	Jim Turnesa	Chick Harbert	Big Spring C.C., Louisville, Ky.	1 up
1953	Walter Burkemo	Felice Torza	Birmingham C.C., Birmingham, Mich.	2 & 1
1954	Chick Harbert	Walter Burkemo	Keller G.C., St. Paul, Minn.	4 & 3
1955	Doug Ford	Cary Middlecoff	Meadowbrook C.C., Detroit, Mich.	4 & 3
1956	Jack Burke	Ted Kroll	Blue Hill C.C., Boston, Mass.	3 & 2
1957	Lionel Hebert	Dow Finsterwald	Miami Valley C.C., Dayton, Ohio	2 & 1
1958	Dow Finsterwald	Billy Casper	Llanerch C.C., Havertown, Pa.	276
1959	Bob Rosburg	Jerry Barber Doug Sanders	Minneapolis G.C., St. Louis Park, Minn.	277
1960	Jay Hebert	Jim Ferrier	Firestone C.C., Akron, Ohio	281
1961	Jerry Barber	Don January	Olympia Fields C.C., Olympia Fields, Ill.	277
1962	Gary Player	Bob Goalby	Aronomink G.C., Newtown Square, Pa.	278
1963	Jack Nicklaus	Dave Ragan, Jnr.	Dallas Athletic Club C.C., Dallas, Tex.	279
1964	Bobby Nichols	Jack Nicklaus Arnold Palmer	Columbus C.C., Columbus, Ohio	271
1965	Dave Marr	Billy Casper Jack Nicklaus	Laurel Valley C.C., Ligonier, Pa.	280
1966	Al Geiberger	Dudley Wysong	Firestone G. & C.C., Akron, Ohio	280
1967	Don January	Don Massengale	Columbine C.C., Littleton, Colo.	281
1968	Julius Boros	Bob Charles Arnold Palmer	Pecan Valley C.C., San Antonio, Tex.	281
1969	Ray Floyd	Gary Player	N.C.R. C.C., Dayton, Ohio	276
1970	Dave Stockton	Arnold Palmer Bob Murphy	Southern Hills C.C., Tulsa, Okla.	279
1971	Jack Nicklaus	Billy Casper	P.G.A. National G.C., Palm Beach Gardens, Fla.	281
1972	Gary Player	Tommy Aaron Jim Jamieson	Oakland Hills, Birmingham, Mich.	281
1973	Jack Nicklaus	Bruce Crampton	Canterbury Golf Club, Cleveland, Ohio	277

Piccadilly World Match-Play

YEAR	WINNER	RUNNER-UP	VENUE	SCORE
1964	Arnold Palmer	N. C. Coles	Wentworth	2 and 1
1965	Gary Player	P. W. Thomson	Wentworth	3 and 2
1966	Gary Player	J. W. Nicklaus	Wentworth	6 and 4
1967	Arnold Palmer	P. W. Thomson	Wentworth	1 hole
1968	Gary Player	R. Charles	Wentworth	1 hole
1969	R. Charles	G. Littler	Wentworth	37th hole
1970	J. W. Nicklaus	L. Trevino	Wentworth	2 and 1
1971	Gary Player	J. W. Nicklaus	Wentworth	5 and 4
1972	Tom Weiskopf	L. Trevino	Wentworth	4 and 3

Tom Weiskopf

Gary Player

Jack Nicklaus

Arnold Palmer

Piccadilly World Match-Play 1972

FIRST ROUND

Peter Oosterhuis defeated Gary Player, 1 up

Player:	Out:	535	633	444 — 37	In:	34c	434	444 — X . . . X
Oosterhuis	Out:	434	425	444 — 34	In:	243	435	456 — 36 . . . 70

Oosterhuis 2 up

Player	Out:	534	434	445 — 36	In:	344	435	455 — 37 . . . 73
Oosterhuis	Out:	524	534	455 — 37	In:	344	535	355 — 37 . . . 74

Tom Weiskopf defeated David Graham, 3 and 2

Graham	Out:	434	434	434 — 33	In:	344	434	55c — X . . . X
Weiskopf	Out:	434	434	444 — 34	In:	343	434	454 — 34 . . . 68

Weiskopf 2 up

Graham	Out:	434	444	443 — 34	In:	344	434	5
Weiskopf	Out:	433	434	534 — 33	In:	344	43c	4

Lee Trevino defeated Doug Sanders, 2 and 1

Trevino	Out:	434	333	544 — 33	In:	346	434	444 — 36 . . . 69
Sanders	Out:	434	424	444 — 33	In:	344	435	456 — 38 . . . 71

Trevino 2 up

revino	Out:	324	434	344 — 31	In:	244	435	55
Sanders	Out:	424	334	444 — 32	In:	344	434	45

Tony Jacklin defeated Grier Jones, 7 and 6

Jacklin	Out:	434	434	445 — 35	In:	335	333	445 — 33 . . . 68
Jones	Out:	435	525	545 — 38	In:	334	444	457 — 38 . . . 76

Jacklin 7 up

Jacklin	Out:	534	434	434 — 37	In:	444	
Jones	Out:	434	544	443 — 35	In:	344	

SECOND ROUND

Weiskopf defeated Oosterhuis, 4 and 3

Oosterhuis	Out:	535	434	544 — 37	In:	444	435	454 — 37 . . . 74
Weiskopf	Out:	435	434	444 — 35	In:	334	435	454 — 35 . . . 70

Weiskopf 4 up

Oosterhuis	Out:	524	444	444 — 35	In:	c44	425
Weiskopf	Out:	435	525	344 — 35	In:	344	434

Trevino defeated Jacklin, 1 up

Trevino	Out:	424	434	353 — 32	In:	433	444	454 — 35 . . . 67
Jacklin	Out:	425	334	544 — 34	In:	25c	436	465 — X . . . X

Trevino 4 up

Trevino	Out:	434	435	444 — 35	In:	243	434	444 — 31 . . . 66
Jacklin	Out:	434	323	433 — 29	In:	334	434	445 — 34 . . . 63

FINAL

Weiskopf defeated Trevino 4 and 3

Weiskopf	Out:	434	334	445 — 34	In:	354	335	455 — 37 . . . 71
Trevino	Out:	534	334	445 — 35	In:	344	435	455 — 37 . . . 72

Weiskopf 1 up

Weiskopf	Out:	433	534	344 — 33	In:	443	435
Trevino	Out:	534	523	445 — 35	In:	354	525

Weiskopf £8,500; Trevino £4,500; Oosterhuis, Jacklin £3,000; Player, Graham, Sanders, Jones £1,500.

Ryder Cup Matches

1927   Worcester, Mass., U.S.A. June 3 and 4
Grand total: Great Britain 2 matches, U.S.A. 9 matches, 1 match halved

1929   Moortown, Leeds. April 26 and 27
Grand total: Great Britain 6 matches, U.S.A. 4 matches, 2 matches halved

1931   Scioto, Columbus, Ohio, U.S.A. June 26 and 27
Grand total: Great Britain 3 matches, U.S.A. 9 matches

1933   Southport and Ainsdale, Southport. June 26 and 27
Grand total: Great Britain 6 matches, U.S.A. 5 matches, 1 match halved

1935   Ridgewood, New Jersey, U.S.A. September 28 and 29
Grand total: Great Britain 2 matches, U.S.A. 8 matches, 2 matches halved

1937   Southport and Ainsdale, Southport. June 29 and 30
Grand total: Great Britain 3 matches, U.S.A. 7 matches, 2 matches halved

1947   Portland, Oregon, U.S.A. November 1 and 2
Grand total: Great Britain 1 match, U.S.A. 11 matches

1949   Ganton, Scarborough. September 16 and 17
Grand total: Great Britain 5 matches, U.S.A. 7 matches

1951   Pinehurst, N.C. U.S.A. November 2–4
Grand total: Great Britain 2 matches, U.S.A. 9 matches, 1 match halved

1953   Wentworth, Virginia Water. October 2 and 3
Grand total: Great Britain 5 matches, U.S.A. 6 matches, 1 match halved

1955   Thunderbird Golf and Country Club, California. November 5 and 6
Grand total: Great Britain 4 matches, U.S.A. 8 matches

1957   Lindrick Golf Club, Leeds, Yorkshire. October 4 and 5
Grand total: Great Britain 7 matches, U.S.A. 4 matches, 1 match halved

1959   Eldorado Country Club, California. November 6 and 7
Grand total: Great Britain 2 matches, U.S.A. 7 matches, 3 matches halved

1961   Royal Lytham and St. Annes. October 14 and 15
Grand total: Great Britain 9 matches, U.S.A. 14 matches, 1 match halved

1963   East Lake Country Club, Atlanta, Georgia. October 11–13
Grand total: Great Britain 9 matches, U.S.A. 23 matches

1965   Royal Birkdale, Southport, Lancashire. October 7–9
Grand total: Great Britain 12 matches, U.S.A. 19 matches, 1 match halved

1967   Champions Golf Club, Houston, Texas. October 20–22
Grand total: Great Britain 8 matches, U.S.A. 23 matches, 1 match halved

1969   Royal Birkdale, Southport, Lancashire. September 18–20
Grand total: Great Britain 16 matches, U.S.A. 16 matches

1971   Old Warson Country Club, St. Louis. September 16–18
Grand total: Great Britain 13 matches, U.S.A. 18 matches, 1 match halved

Walker Cup Matches

1922 National Links, Long Island. August 29
Grand total: Great Britain 4 matches, U.S.A. 8 matches

1923 St. Andrews. May 19
Grand total: Great Britain 5 matches, U.S.A. 6 matches, 1 match halved

1924 Garden City, New York. September 12 and 13
Grand total: Great Britain 3 matches, U.S.A. 9 matches

1926 St. Andrews. June 2 and 3
Grand total: Great Britain 5 matches, U.S.A. 6 matches, 1 match halved

1928 Chicago Golf Club, Wheaton, U.S.A. August 30 and 31
Grand total: Great Britain 1 match, U.S.A. 11 matches

1930 Royal St. George's Sandwich. May 15 and 16
Grand total: Great Britain 2 matches, U.S.A. 10 matches

1932 Brooklyn, Mass. September 1 and 2
Grand total: Great Britain 1 match, U.S.A. 8 matches, 3 matches halved

1934 St. Andrews. May 11 and 12
Grand total: Great Britain 2 matches, U.S.A. 9 matches, 1 match halved

1936 Pine Valley. September 2 and 3
Grand total: Great Britain 0 matches, U.S.A. 9 matches, 3 matches halved

1938 St. Andrews. June 3 and 4
Grand total: Great Britain 7 matches, U.S.A. 4 matches, 1 match halved

1947 St. Andrews. May 16 and 17
Grand total: Great Britain 4 matches, U.S.A. 8 matches

1949 Winged Foot, New York. August 19 and 20
Grand total: Great Britain 2 matches, U.S.A. 10 matches

1951 Royal Birkdale, Southport, Lancashire. May 11 and 12
Grand total: Great Britain 3 matches, U.S.A. 6 matches, 3 matches halved

1953 Marion, Mass. September 4 and 5
Grand total: Great Britain 3 matches, U.S.A. 9 matches

1955 St. Andrews. May 20 and 21
Grand total: Great Britain 2 matches, U.S.A. 10 matches

1957 Minikahda. September 1 and 2
Grand total: Great Britain 3 matches, U.S.A. 8 matches, 1 match halved

1959 Muirfield. May 15 and 16
Grand total: Great Britain 3 matches, U.S.A. 9 matches

1961 Seattle. September 1 and 2
Grand total: Great Britain 1 match, U.S.A. 11 matches

1963 Turnberry. May 24 and 25
Grand total: Great Britain 8 matches, U.S.A. 12 matches, 4 matches halved

1965 Baltimore, U.S.A. September 3 and 4
Grand total: Great Britain 11 matches, U.S.A. 11 matches, 2 matches halved

1967 Royal St. Georges, Sandwich. May 19 and 20
Grand total: Great Britain 7 matches, U.S.A. 13 matches, 4 matches halved

1969 Milwaukee, U.S.A. August 22 and 23
Grand total: Great Britain 8 matches, U.S.A. 10 matches, 6 matches halved

1971 St. Andrews. May 26 and 27
Grand total: Great Britain 13 matches, U.S.A. 11 matches

British Amateur Championship

YEAR	WINNER	RUNNER-UP	VENUE	SCORE
1885	A. F. MacFie	H. G. Hutchinson	Hoylake	7 and 6
1886	H. G. Hutchinson	Henry Lamb	St. Andrews	7 and 6
1887	H. G. Hutchinson	John Ball	Hoylake	1 hole
1888	John Ball	J. E. Laidlay	Prestwick	5 and 4
1889	J. E. Laidlay	L. M. B. Melville	St. Andrews	2 and 1
1890	John Ball	J. E. Laidlay	Hoylake	4 and 3
1891	J. E. Laidlay	H. H. Hilton	St. Andrews	20th hole
1892	John Ball	H. H. Hilton	Sandwich	3 and 1
1893	Peter Anderson	J. E. Laidlay	Prestwick	1 hole
1894	John Ball	S. M. Fergusson	Hoylake	1 hole
1895	L. M. B. Melville	John Ball	St. Andrews	19th hole
1896*	F. G. Talt	H. H. Hilton	Sandwich	8 and 7

* Thirty-six holes played on and after this date

YEAR	WINNER	RUNNER-UP	VENUE	SCORE
1897	A. J. T. Allan	James Robb	Muirfield	4 and 2
1898	F. G. Tait	S. M. Fergusson	Hoylake	7 and 5
1899	John Ball	F. G. Tait	Prestwick	37th hole
1900	H. H. Hilton	James Robb	Sandwich	8 and 7
1901	H. H. Hilton	J. L. Low	St. Andrews	1 hole
1902	C. Hutchings	S. H. Fry	Hoylake	1 hole
1903	R. Maxwell	H. G. Hutchinson	Muirfield	6 and 5
1904	W. J. Travis, U.S.A.	Ed. Blackwell	Sandwich	4 and 3
1905	A. G. Barry	Hon. O. Scott	Prestwick	3 and 2
1906	James Robb	C. C. Lingen	Hoylake	4 and 3
1907	John Ball	C. A. Palmer	St. Andrews	6 and 4
1908	E. A. Lassen	H. E. Taylor	Sandwich	7 and 6
1909	R. Maxwell	Capt. C. K. Hutchison	Muirfield	1 hole
1910	John Ball	C. Aylmer	Hoylake	10 and 9
1911	H. H. Hilton	E. A. Lassen	Prestwick	4 and 3
1912	John Ball	Abe Mitchell	Westward Ho!	38th hole
1913	H. H. Hilton	R. Harris	St. Andrews	6 and 5
1914	J. L. C. Jenkins	C. O. Hezlet	Sandwich	3 and 2
1920	C. J. H. Tolley	R. A. Gardner, U.S.A.	Muirfield	37th hole
1921	W. I. Hunter	A. J. Graham	Hoylake	12 and 11
1922	E. W. E. Holderness	J. Caven	Prestwick	1 hole
1923	R. H. Wethered	R. Harris	Deal	7 and 6
1924	E. W. E. Holderness	E. F. Storey	St. Andrews	3 and 2
1925	Robert Harris	K. F. Fradgley	Westward Ho!	13 and 12
1926	Jesse Sweetser, U.S.A.	A. F. Simpson	Muirfield	6 and 5
1927	Dr. W. Tweddell	D. E. Landale	Hoylake	7 and 6
1928	T. P. Perkins	R. H. Wethered	Prestwick	6 and 4
1929	C. J. H. Tolley	J. N. Smith	Sandwich	4 and 3
1930	R. T. Jones, U.S.A.	R. H. Wethered	St. Andrews	7 and 6
1931	Eric Martin Smith	J. De Forest	Westward Ho!	1 hole
1932	J. De Forest	E. W. Fiddian	Muirfield	3 and 1
1933	Hon. M. Scott	T. A. Bourn	Hoylake	4 and 3
1934	W. Lawson Little, U.S.A.	J. Wallace	Prestwick	14 and 13
1935	W. Lawson Little, U.S.A.	Dr. W. Tweddell	Royal Lytham and St. Annes	1 hole
1936	H. Thomson	J. Ferrier, Australia	St. Andrews	2 holes
1937	R. Sweeney, Jnr., U.S.A.	L. O. Munn	Sandwich	3 and 2
1938	C. R. Yates, U.S.A.	R. C. Ewing	Troon	3 and 2
1939	A. T. Kyle	A. A. Duncan	Hoylake	2 and 1
1946	J. Bruen	R. Sweeney, U.S.A.	Birkdale	4 and 3
1947	W. P. Turnesa, U.S.A.	R. D. Chapman, U.S.A.	Carnoustie	3 and 2
1948	F. R. Stranahan, U.S.A.	C. Stowe	Sandwich	5 and 4
1949	S. M. M'Cready	W. P. Turnesa, U.S.A.	Portmarnock	2 and 1
1950	F. R. Stranahan, U.S.A.	R. D. Chapman, U.S.A.	St. Andrews	8 and 6
1951	R. D. Chapman, U.S.A.	C. R. Coe, U.S.A.	Porthcawl	5 and 4
1952	E. H. Ward, U.S.A.	F. R. Stranahan, U.S.A.	Prestwick	6 and 5

1953	J. B. Carr	E. Harvie Ward, U.S.A.	Hoylake	2 holes
1954	D. W. Bachll, Australia	W. C. Campbell, U.S.A.	Muirfield	2 and 1
1955	J. W. Conrad, U.S.A.	A. Slater	Royal Lytham and St. Annes	3 and 2
1956*	J. C. Beharrell	L. G. Taylor	Troon	5 and 4
1957*	R. Reid Jack	H. B. Ridgley, U.S.A.	Formby	2 and 1

* In 1956 and 1957 the quarter-finals, semi-finals and final were played over 36 holes

1958*	J. B. Carr	A. Thirlwell	St. Andrews	3 and 2

* In 1958, semi-finals and finals only were played over 36 holes

1959	D. R. Beman, U.S.A.	W. Hyndman, U.S.A.	Sandwich	3 and 2
1960	J. B. Carr	R. Cochran, U.S.A.	Portrush	8 and 7
1961	M. F. Bonallack	J. Walker	Turnberry	6 and 4
1962	R. D. Davies, U.S.A.	J. Povall	Hoylake	1 hole
1963	M. S. R. Lunt	J. G. Blackwell	St. Andrews	2 and 1
1964	Gordon J. Clark	M. S. R. Lunt	Ganton	39th hole
1965	M. F. Bonallack	C. A. Clark	Porthcawl	2 and 1
1966	R. E. Cole, S. Africa	R. D. B. M. Shade	Carnoustie (18 holes)	3 and 2
1967	R. B. Dickson, U.S.A.	R. J. Cerrudo, U.S.A.	Formby	2 and 1
1968	M. F. Bonallack	J. B. Carr	Troon	7 and 6
1969	M. F. Bonallack	W. Hyndman, U.S.A.	Hoylake	3 and 2
1970	M. F. Bonallack	W. Hyndman, U.S.A.	Newcastle Co. Down	8 and 7
1971	S. Melnyk, U.S.A.	J. Simmons, U.S.A.	Carnoustie	3 and 2
1972	T. Homer	A. Thirlwell	R. St. George's	5 and 3
1973	R. Siderowf, U.S.A.	P. Moody	Royal Porthcawl	5 and 3

American Amateur Championship

YEAR	WINNER	RUNNER-UP	VENUE	BY
1893	W. G. Lawrence	C. B. Macdonald	Newport, R.I.	4 and 3
1894	L. B. Stoddart	C. B. Macdonald	St. Andrews	5 and 4
1895	C. B. Macdonald	C. Sands	Newport, R.I.	12 and 11
1896	H. J. Whigham	J. G. Thorp	Shinnecock	8 and 3
1897	H. J. Whigham	W. R. Betts	Wheaton, Ill.	8 and 2
1898	Finlay S. Douglas	W. B. Smith	Morris County	5 and 7
1899	H. M. Harriman	F. S. Douglas	Onwentsia	3 and 6
1900	W. J. Travis	F. S. Douglas	Garden City	2 holes
1901	W. J. Travis	W. E. Egan	Atlantic City	5 and 4
1902	Louis N. James	E. M. Byers	Glen View	4 and 3
1903	W. J. Travis	E. M. Byers	Nassau	4 and 3
1904	H. Chandler Egan	F. Herreschoff	Baltusrol	8 and 6
1905	H. Chandler Egan	D. E. Sawyer	Wheaton, Ill.	6 and 5
1906	E. M. Byers	Geo. S. Lyon	Englewood	2 holes
1907	Jerome D. Travers	Arch. Graham	Cleveland	6 and 5
1908	Jerome D. Travers	Max H. Behr	Midlothian, Ill.	8 and 7
1909	R. Gardner	H. C. Egan	Wheaton, Ill.	4 and 4
1910	W. C. Fowness, Jnr.	W. K. Wood	Brookline	4 and 3
1911	H. H. Hilton	F. Herreschoff	Apawamis	37th hole
1912	Jerome D. Travers	Charles Evans	Wheaton, Ill.	7 and 6

American Amateur Championship – continued

YEAR	WINNER	RUNNER-UP	VENUE	BY
1913	Jerome D. Travers	J. G. Anderson	Garden City	6 and 4
1914	F. Ouimet	J. D. Travers	Ekwanok	6 and 5
1915	R. A. Gardner	J. G. Anderson	Detroit	5 and 4
1916	Charles Evans	R. A. Gardner	Merion	4 and 3
1919	D. Heron	R. T. Jones	Oakmont	5 and 4
1920	C. Evans	F. Ouimet	Engineers Club	5 and 4
1921	J. Guildford	Robert Gardner	St. Louis, Clayton	7 and 6
1922	J. Sweetser	Charles Evans	Brookline	3 and 2
1923	Max Marston	Jesse Sweetser	Flossmoor	38th hole
1924	R. T. Jones, Jnr.	G. von Elm	Merton	9 and 8
1925	R. T. Jones, Jnr.	W. Gunn	Oakmont	8 and 7
1926	G. von Elm	R. T. Jones	Baltusrol	2 and 1
1927	R. T. Jones, Jnr.	C. Evans	Minikahda	8 and 7
1928	R. T. Jones, Jnr.	T. P. Perkins	Brae Burn	10 and 9
1929	H. R. Johnston	Dr. O. F. Willing	Del Monte	4 and 3
1930	R. T. Jones, Jnr.	E. V. Homans	Merion	8 and 7
1931	F. Ouimet	J. Westland	Beverley	6 and 5
1932	C. R. Somerville	J. Goodman	Baltimore	2 and 1
1933	G. T. Dunlap	M. R. Marston	Kenwood	6 and 5
1934	W. Lawson Little	D. Goldman	Brookline	8 and 7
1935	W. Lawson Little	W. Emery	Cleveland	4 and 2
1936	J. Fischer	J. M'Lean	Garden City	87 hole
1937	J. Goodman	R. Billows	Portland	2 holes
1938	W. P. Tarnesa	B. P. Abbott	Oakmont	8 and 7
1939	M. H. Ward	R. Billows	Glenview	7 and 5
1940	R. D. Chapman	W. B. McCullough	Winged Foot	11 and 9
1941	M. H. Ward	B. P. Abbott	Omaha	4 and 3
1946	S. E. Bishop	S. Quick	Baltusrol	37th hole
1947	R. H. Riegel	J. Dawson	Pebble Beach	2 and 1
1948	W. P. Turnesa	R. Billows	Memphis	2 and 1
1949	C. R. Coe	Rufus King	Rochester	11 and 10
1950	S. Urzetta	F. R. Stranahan	Minneapolis	39th hole
1951	W. J. Maxwell	J. Cagliardi	Saucon Valley, Pa.	4 and 8
1952	J. Westland	A. Mengert	Seattle	3 and 2
1953	G. Littler	D. Morey	Oklahoma City	1 hole
1954	A. Palmer	R. Sweeney	Detroit	1 hole
1955	E. Harvie Ward	W. Hyndman	Richmond, Va.	9 and 8
1956	E. Harvie Ward	C. Kocsis	Lake Forest, Ill.	5 and 4
1957	H. Robbins	Dr. F. Taylor	Brookline	5 and 4
1958	C. Coe	T. Aaron	San Francisco	5 and 4
1959	J. H. Nicklaus	C. R. Coe	Broadmoor	1 hole
1960	D. R. Beman	R. Gardner	St. Louis, Miss.	6 and 4
1961	J. H. Nicklaus	D. Wsong	Pebble Beach	8 and 6
1962	L. E. Harris, Jnr.	D. Gray	Pinehurst	1 hole
1963	D. R. Beman	D. Sikes	Des Moines	2 and 1
1964	W. Campbell	E. Tutwiler	Canterbury, Ohio	1 hole
1965	R. Murphy	R. Dickson	Tulsa, Okla.	291
1966	G. Cowan, Canada	D. R. Beman	Ardmore, Penn.	285
1967	R. Dickson	Marvin Giles	Colorado	285
1968	B. Fleisher	Marvin Giles	Columbus	284
1969	S. Melnyk	Marvin Giles	Oakmont	286
1970	L. Wadkins	T. Kite	Portland	280
1971	G. Cowan, Canada	E. Pierce	Wilmington	280
1972	M. Giles	B. Crenshaw	Charlotte	288